PHANTOM IN THE RIVER

The Flight of Linfield Two Zero One

GARY WAYNE FOSTER

HELLGATE PRESS   ASHLAND, OREGON

PHANTOM IN THE RIVER

©2010 Gary Wayne Foster

Published by Hellgate Press

Hellgate Press
PO Box 3531
Ashland, OR 97520

email: info@hellgatepress.com

Editor: Janet Mehl
In-house editor: Harley B. Patrick
Cover design: L. Redding

Library of Congress Cataloging-in-Publication Data

Foster, Gary Wayne, 1948-
 Phantom in the river : the flight of Linfield two zero one / Gary Wayne
Foster. -- 1st ed.
   p. cm.
 ISBN 978-1-55571-664-6
 1. Vietnam War, 1961-1975--Campaigns--Vietnam--Thanh Hóa. 2. Vietnam
War, 1961-1975--Aerial operations, American. 3. Southwick, Charles Everett,
1931- 4. Rollins, David John, 1931- 5. Phantom II (Jet fighter plane) 6.
Vietnam War, 1961-1975--Prisoners and prisons--North Vietnamese. 7.
Prisoners of war--United States--Biography. I. Title.
 DS557.8.T47F67 2009
 959.704'345--dc22

                      2009048141

Printed and bound in the United States of America
First edition 10 9 8 7 6 5 4 3 2 1

I dedicate this book to Charles Everett Southwick and David John Rollins; and also to my father, John William Foster, who never flew a fighter jet but knew how to design one.

PHANTOM IN THE RIVER

The Flight of Linfield Two Zero One

Contents

Acknowledgments

THE PHYSICAL ORIGINS OF THE STORY OF THE flight of Linfield Two Zero One are found in Hanoi, Vietnam with the wreckage of a U.S. Navy F-4B Phantom II jet fighter. Official and unofficial written documents provide much of the historical background for the narration. I found, however, that informational gaps existed. Personal and telephone interviews filled those gaps. The interviews not only corrected informational deficiencies, they provided color that is lost in official records. As time progressed, I became more knowledgeable about the topics. I learned how to ask better questions or seek specific facts. After awhile, information became abundant. Gradually, over a long period of time, using the information obtained from so many sources, the story came together.

I wish to acknowledge those who assisted me along the way with this project:

First and foremost are Captain (CAPT) Charles Everett Southwick, U.S. Navy (Ret.) and Commander (CDR) David John Rollins, U.S. Navy (Ret.) both of whom ironically go by nicknames derived from their middle names: Ev and Jack. I know at times I amused or perhaps annoyed each of them as I tried to understand each intricate detail of the flight of Linfield Two Zero One. While my questions proved salient to my understanding, to Ev and Jack, many of them may have seemed naïve. Their lively, sometimes pointed comments about the draft manuscripts resulted in necessary revisions but strengthened the story. To Ev and Jack, I offer my deepest personal thanks.

Additionally, I want to thank Vice Admiral (VADM) Edward H. Martin, U.S. Navy (Ret.), VADM Joseph Mobley, U.S. Navy (Ret.), both of whom are graduates of the United States Naval Academy, and Rear Admiral (RADM) Hugh Dennis (Denny) Wisely, U.S. Navy (Ret.). Each individual provided me with a wealth of information about aircraft carrier operations and naval aviation.

Lieutenant (LT) Patrick McKenna, a current Navy F-18 Super Hornet pilot who flew with VFA-27 (Royal Maces) off the USS *Kitty Hawk* (now CV-63) and who made the first catapult launch from and trap (landing) aboard the USS *George H. W. Bush* (CVN-77), proved an invaluable resource about flight deck operations on the *Kitty Hawk*.

I received helpful information from Fred Metz, Paul Mather, Joe Forester, Danny Kolipano, Alexander Wattay, Raymond Merritt, and Richard Horne.

I offer my thanks to John D. Sherwood, historian and writer at the Naval History and Heritage Command, who guided me through my research efforts of the U.S. Navy archives. I thank Mr. Peter Vankevich of the Copyright Office and Ms. Mari Nakahara, Ph.D., of the Asia Reading Room, both at the U.S. Library of Congress in Washington, D.C., and Master Sergeant (MSG) Lisa K. Sutton of the Missouri Air National Guard. I am grateful to the Tailhook Association for allowing me to use its library and files; the Arizona Wing of the Commemorative Air Force in Mesa, Arizona; Scott Fenholm of the Dahlberg Aviation Research Center and the Museum of Flight, both in Seattle, Washington. I also thank the U.S. Navy Memorial Foundation in Washington, D.C.; Frank McNally and the docents of the Smithsonian Institution National Air and Space Museum in Chantilly, Virginia; Robert Rasmussen (Director), Hill Goodspeed, Phil and Maureen Duryea and Jim Butler and the other volunteers (docents) of the National Naval Aviation Museum at the U.S. Naval Air Station in Pensacola, Florida; the National Museum of the U.S. Air Force at Wright-Patterson Air Force Base in Dayton, Ohio; the Pima Air and Space Museum n Tucson, Arizona; the San Diego Air and Space Museum in San Diego, California; and Rick Harris and Mike Robinson of the Collings Foundation Houston Volunteers who gave me a walk-around tour of the Foundation's restored F-4D Phantom II at Ellington Field, southeast of Houston, Texas.

I would like to thank Bill Liegois for his advice on operational aspects of jet engines; Barry Butler, Dean of the College of Engineering at the University of Iowa, for his review of the section on compressor stall; Jim Kill and Al Austin (now deceased), Professor of Civil Engineering at Iowa State University, for their advice on truss bridge design; Robert Destatte and Ron Ward for their translation assistance; and Jason Chudy, public affairs officer (now retired) of the USS *Kitty Hawk,* who provided me with details about the ship.

Through Bonnie Barkey Moore, I want to express my sincerest gratitude to Herman D. Barkey, who I was privileged to meet in late summer 2002, who sat with me for two hours in his home near St. Louis and kept me completely entranced with stories about the development and design of the F-4 Phantom II.

I thank the staff of the USS *Yorktown* (CV-10) in Charleston, South Carolina and the docents (of which Ev Southwick is one) of the USS *Midway* Museum (CV-41) in San Diego, California.

Across the Atlantic in the United Kingdom, Eric Thomas of the Martin-Baker Aircraft Company provided support and insightful information about the Mark 5 ejection seat. Chris Hobson, of the Royal Air Force Staff College at Bracknell and past head librarian at the Joint Services Command and Staff College at Shrivenham, aided me with my research efforts. I thank the Institute of Civil Engineers (ICE), London (Westminster), United Kingdom, which provided research assistance on the Warren truss; The Imperial War Museum in London; and Les Archives Nationale d'Outre Mer in Aix-en-Provence, France, which provided me with research assistance about the French design of the original arched bridge at Thanh Hoa and the Hanoi-to-Saigon railway. I also thank Istvan Toperczer for his assistance from Hungary.

On the far side of the Pacific, it was a great pleasure to sit in Hanoi in the living room of Nguyen Dinh Doan (pronounced, *when ding zwan*) a civil (structural) engineer, who told me about the design and construction of the Ham Rong Bridge, the same bridge the Americans called the Thanh Hoa Bridge.

I wish to thank Ngo Thi Tuyen (pronounced, *no tea twin*), the Heroine of Thanh Hoa; Nguyen Anh (pronounced, *when ang*), Curator (now retired) of the Vietnam Air Force and Air Defense Museum in Hanoi; Nguyen Ngoc Tran (pronounced, *when niop tran*), Director General of Project Management Unit No. 85 (now retired as National Hero) in Vinh; and my friend Hoang Tran Dung (pronounced, *whong tran zoong*), in Hanoi, each for providing me with much background information about the air defenses of North Vietnam, the North Vietnamese transportation system and the Thanh Hoa Bridge. The military museum in Thanh Hoa helped me to understand the air defense of the Thanh Hoa Bridge.

I thank Matsaaki Hayakawa and Isamu Yatsuhashi, both living in Japan, for their research assistance.

No one can research and write a book, however long or short, without the moral support of others. In this regard, it would be an oversight not to mention those who encouraged me forward with this book. I offer my thanks to my father, John William Foster, whose enthusiasm for the project became apparent as he accompanied me while scouring through aircraft junk yards in Tucson, Arizona in an attempt to learn more about the F-4; Carol Bolton, my sister, and her husband, Tom Bolton; Ginger Haden, my cousin, and her husband, Don Haden; John Pessoni, the Rev. Ray Stubbe, Bob Arrotta, Tommy Eichler and Mike Archer, each of whom are veterans of Khe Sanh;

Donna Elliott, who lost her brother Jerry in 1968 during the siege of Khe Sanh; Dennis Mannion, also a veteran of Khe Sanh, his wife, Joan, and sons Jake, Blake and Devin; Richard Hoar and Stacey Sash Schildroth each for their literary critique and suggestions; and John Keay (famous Scottish writer and historian). I also thank good friends Jane and Chuck Zaloudek; Gary, Betty Jo, Jessie and Krista DeBusschere; Tailen Mak; Gene Wilkie; Lee Humiston, Managing Director and Curator of the Maine Military Museum and Learning Center in South Portland, Maine, and his wife, Maureen; Micheal C. Webb and his wife, Donna; Jim and Karen Keys; Kathy and Tom Bankhead; Kevin McCauley; Tim Edwards; Dick Hutmacher; Bob Hoffmann; Mike McKenna; Bruce O'Connor; Bob Rusch; Bill Harper; Bob Haskins; Dimy and Pascale Doresca; Bill Jones; and Alan Palmer.

I would be remiss if I didn't acknowledge those who, while not involved with this nine-year writing effort, provided support merely through their friendship: Steve and Mary Teraberry, Elmer and Thelma Bloom, Lori Schoening, Steve Allchin, Chris Broders, Lynn Pruitt, Melanie Koch, Henry Marquard, I.L. Ravanna (Isle of Jura), Eric Martin (nephew), Christie Martin (niece), Larry Guarino, Le Tran Ngoc (translator, Hanoi), Herb Ohrt, Jennifer Bowlin, David J. Meloy, Mo Keane, Julia and Grace Sturms, Justin Edwards and his wife Katja, Prasad (PK) Datta (Sanchi), Sunil Choudhury (Bhojpur) and Darla Sterner. Thanks to all.

Preface

THE WAR IN VIETNAM—THE LONGEST RUNNING war in United States history—ended with the fall of Saigon to the North Vietnamese in the spring of 1975. Bitterly fought, collectively, antagonists though they were, the United States of America and the Socialist Republic of Vietnam, more commonly known then as North Vietnam, mobilized millions of people to fight in a country not quite the size of California. The United States, in particular, ordered the might of its air force to Southeast Asia and its aircraft carrier force to the Gulf of Tonkin to compromise the war-making capabilities of North Vietnam. Bolstered by support from Russia and China and other Soviet Bloc countries, North Vietnam fought back.

History often conceals the underlying accumulation of solitary accounts that, randomly or not, contribute to a larger, overall event. Sadly, many of these "small" accounts are often ignored, discarded as unimportant or perceived to be of little value. A staggering number, more than three thousand U.S. fixed wing aircraft were lost during the Vietnam War. Each incident, subsumed by the larger statistic, has a story.

This story, based on real events, salvages an isolated incident from the scrapheap of untold mini-histories. Condensed, the story is simple. On 14 May 1967, two American Navy airmen, Charles Everett "Ev" Southwick and David John "Jack" Rollins, launched from the USS *Kitty Hawk* in their F-4B Phantom II aircraft. They did not return to their carrier.

Intentionally unburdened with jargon or military rhetoric or vernacular, technical descriptions and details necessary for the reader to understand various situations or circumstances are explained in basic terms. To reach beyond these fundamental explanations would mire the story and encumber it too much. I have speculated only where prudent or where such speculation can be reasonably deduced from research or others' accounts. While any mistakes found are mine alone, I argue the essence of this story should be neither lost nor forgotten.

Gary Wayne Foster
Muscatine, Iowa

Chapter 1
Phantom in the River

ON BOARD THE USS *KITTY HAWK*, maneuvering in the Gulf of Tonkin on a Sunday in mid-May 1967, F-4 Phantom IIs and other American combat aircraft of Air Wing Eleven were being readied for another day of strikes against targets in North Vietnam.

The USS *Kitty Hawk*, with the number "63" heroically emblazoned on each side of her tall island, was one of four United States attack aircraft carriers operating in or transiting to or from the Gulf of Tonkin at that time. She and her air wing were nearing the end of a second combat cruise. *Kitty Hawk* and her air wing, having arrived in the Gulf just after Thanksgiving 1966, had seen their fair share of the air war over North Vietnam. They were scheduled to return to San Diego within a few weeks.

Meanwhile, on land, as *Kitty Hawk* steamed off the coast below the horizon, the sleepy town of Thanh Hoa, situated on the banks of the Song Ma, went about its daily business. Accustomed to its unspoken role of guardian for more than hundreds of years, Thanh Hoa protected a narrow isthmus in the Song Ma. Across this isthmus, which constricted the flow of the muddy waters that spilled from the hinterlands of North Vietnam toward the Gulf of Tonkin, sat a steel structure that connected the opposite banks. The structure was known as Cau Ham Rong.

The air this day, unusually clear, was heavy with humidity that sapped the strength of the villagers who worked in the fields or along the riverbank. The sun, now past its apex, beat its relentless heat down on the quiet streets and empty buildings of Thanh Hoa. Its rays bounced off the earth, causing heat waves in the air to distort shapes and make them shimmer in the distance across the surrounding rice paddies. The foliage of the lush vegetation was transformed into deep verdant hues by the mid-afternoon sun as its light glinted off the translucent greenery. Adding to the pastoral scene, big black water buffalo marched ponderously across the soggy paddies pulling plows as their masters walked behind them in the black soil.

Offering some relief, a gentle breeze blew in from the sea causing the bright green fronds of the tall palm trees to sway wistfully. The soft hum and the lazy, alluring rustle emanating from the wild bamboo stands at the edges of the rice paddies could be heard throughout the flatland. These soothing sounds seemed not to disrupt but rather to enhance the pervasive silence along the Song Ma.

Nguyen Minh Huan (pronounced, *when ming whan*) and his longtime companion Ho Van Phong (pronounced, *ho van fong*) sat on their haunches—the crouching position typical of Asians—in the shade of a tree downstream of Thanh Hoa. They could see the other side of the river clearly. Sometimes the atmosphere was so opaque that only the outlines of the trees in the distance could be discerned. Not this day. The clear atmosphere provided a grand panorama of the river valley's flat, sweeping terrain. The geographic details on the opposite bank were clearly distinguishable and Nguyen could make out the hull of a boat that had been abandoned across the river many years before. He could see small fishing dugout canoes being paddled against the current while other small boats floated lazily downstream in the opposite direction. The shadows of a few billowy, white clouds danced across the river as the clouds passed overhead.

It was a quiet afternoon. Nguyen and Ho, relishing a break from the endless toils of plying the Song Ma in their boats, relaxed and enjoyed their hand-rolled cigarettes.

Nguyen had walked to this spot along the levee from his home for a moment of respite from the close quarters of his village and to meet Ho whose small boat was moored not far away. The services of both men and their boats were required often to provide river transportation for the replenishment of munitions for the antiaircraft guns at Cau Ham Rong. They would pick up ammunition from some point down river and ferry it upriver to the air defense crews where, at some hidden landing, the cargo would be offloaded from the boats. Many times the boats were so heavily laden that there were only a few inches of freeboard. Replenishment was usually performed late at night. But Nguyen had been relieved of his duty the night before. He hoped this break would continue for a few days. He could rest and perform badly needed maintenance on his boat.

The two friends exchanged stories of the previous week and reminisced about events from years past, such as the time Ho Chi Minh (pronounced, *ho chee ming*) had visited Thanh Hoa and had dedicated the new Cau Ham Rong on his birthday in May of 1964.

Ho, who enjoyed having the same name as the leader of his country, had arrived from Sam Son, located near the mouth of the river, to pick up some military cargo just downstream of Thanh Hoa. Pressed for time, Ho explained to Nguyen that he needed to leave; he was running late and he needed to conceal his boat from view during the rest of the day. Ho rose from his crouching position and walked to his boat. Nguyen watched as he unmoored the craft and started the tiny engine. The old wood craft floated away and then, as the motor labored, made its way upstream.

While watching his old friend depart, Nguyen thought about his childhood, about his own children, who were now grown with kids of their own and about the days when he and Ho had fought the French. Now they found themselves in the middle of a new war. Sadly for Nguyen, he and his friend were too old to fight; but they did what they could.

Nguyen enjoyed watching the river and the flat scenery around him that was his homeland. He never tired of the serenity of the Song Ma. Nguyen had lived on the banks of the Song Ma his entire life. He enjoyed the easy setting of the area, the soft scenery around Thanh Hoa and the calming effects of the river. Nguyen loved it; he knew no other life and was perfectly content.

Nguyen's ancestors, having arrived from the environs of Hanoi hundreds of years before, had passed down lore and had taught the trades of the river. Each generation learned about the river and the life that it shaped for its inhabitants. Nguyen's father had worked on the river, carrying sand in barges to Thanh Hoa and to smaller villages farther up the river. Sometimes he ferried giant logs, which had been felled in the mountains, down the river to waiting ships bound for distant, foreign destinations.

Nguyen had used the river knowledge and navigational skills he had gained from his father in the war for independence against the French. He had also learned river trading from his father and he had become an astute negotiator.

Nguyen and his extended family lived in a small three-room home with a low ceiling and a tiny kitchen in the back. Their home was situated on the perimeter of a small square in a village on the backside of the levee that protected the village from the floods of the Song Ma. Constructed over many decades, perhaps as long ago as a hundred years, the levee was maintained and strengthened by the local inhabitants every year.

Nguyen owned some chickens and some small pigs and a small parcel of property nearby on which he grew rice. His two water buffalo nourished his family and allowed him to take his meager products to market in nearby Thanh Hoa. But because of the American air attacks around Thanh Hoa, and the government decree that the town's citizenry should take refuge in the hills, the population of Thanh Hoa fell as did the daily and weekly market activity.

Content in his solitude, Nguyen now sat alone contemplating the calm beauty of the Song Ma as it glided silently past him.

While Nguyen enjoyed the serenity of this lazy afternoon, not far away, to the northwest, in the direction of Cau Ham Rong, a portentous event was unfolding. The tranquility of Nguyen's surroundings was shattered. It began with the roaring, resonating sound of jet aircraft.

Startled, Nguyen knew the pride of his region, the symbol of Thanh Hoa, was under attack again. The Americans were trying to destroy Cau Ham Rong, the very bridge that Ho Chi Minh had dedicated just three years before. Nguyen, still crouching, saw American airplanes streak through the skies toward the bridge from the north. He heard the screaming of the jets, flying at steep, downward angles, their engines trailing black exhaust, as they dived for the bridge. He could see small puffs of white and black smoke, suspended motionless, dotting the sky. The antiaircraft guns that protected the bridge were in heavy action, leaving a trail marked by these small puffs of smoke.

Nguyen heard the sharp explosions of the multiple-impact of rockets. The rockets, as they flew toward their targets, left behind their telltale trail of smoke. After the planes from the north had passed, the horizon filled with thick smoke that rose but did not seem to drift away. Almost immediately, more planes, this time from the south, dived earthward and then, briefly hidden by the smoke, would reappear in a steep climb north of Thanh Hoa. Nguyen heard the deeper, rumbling, attenuated explosions of bombs, like muted thunder, rolling across the paddies. The explosions increased in tempo and with such intensity that it seemed they might never cease. More greasy, black smoke broiled angrily into the sky. Nguyen's world was coming undone.

Nguyen, being so far away from Cau Ham Rong and Thanh Hoa, perceived he was in no danger and continued to rest on his haunches. He watched the smoke rise above the horizon, obscuring his vision of the mountains far behind the bridge. He surmised that he and his river barge, one of the largest on the river, would be in demand to deliver munitions to the defenders of Cau Ham Rong and to bring out the wounded. If this was a big strike, he knew his services would be called on again soon, probably that very night. Nguyen knew the break he needed would be postponed. He would be ready.

Then, out of the corner of his eye, Nguyen caught sight of something huge, something strange, coming toward him, flying through the lazy afternoon sky. It seemed like a big, black prehistoric bird, but as it came closer, he knew it was a *may bay my* (American airplane). It loomed large and threatening. For an instant, Nguyen thought he was being attacked. But, he reasoned, why would an American jet attack an old man sitting beneath a tree smoking a hand-rolled cigarette? Not alarmed, but with his gaze now fixed on the monster zooming toward him, Nguyen remained motionless and watched. The aircraft trailed dark smoke and made shrill, metallic, grinding sounds. The sun's bright afternoon rays bounced off the angles and surfaces of the plane, making it difficult to recognize any distinct feature.

Nguyen had seen only the wreckages of American planes, never an undamaged one, and never up close—nothing like this. The foreboding plane was knifing through the air toward him, growing in ominous size as it approached. The plane flew so low, just above the horizon, that it seemed to Nguyen he could reach up and touch it. Making its frightening, whirring sound, the monstrous jet was closing the distance to Nguyen with astonishing speed. It seemed first to be flying south, then it angled a little more easterly, and finally southeast directly at him.

Suddenly, Nguyen heard and saw explosions in the top of the plane as it passed just over the tops of some trees. He watched in awe as dark objects were thrust upward from it; two bundles hurling into space. Almost immediately, he caught a momentary glimpse of the blossoming of what he knew to be a parachute just above the ground. But while Nguyen knew a man was suspended beneath the parachute, his eyes did not follow the fleeting image. He was too captivated by the enormity of the American plane that was now streaking through the air at treetop level with its horrifying, growling noise.

Nguyen stood immediately to his feet. The sinister-looking American warplane kept coming at him, almost severing the treetops, its shadow ripping across the ground. Nguyen was fixated. He could not take his eyes off the aircraft as it flew directly overhead and downstream away from him, its noise growing then fading. Watching the underside of the American air giant, Nguyen noted the width and angularity of its large wings and the cylindrical protrusions beneath them, the odd juxtaposition of the trailing smaller wings, the large, round, pointed elongated tube beneath its fuselage, and the black smoke that trailed from the darkened tail. The plane's rich exhaust, repugnant to Nguyen's senses, immediately settled down through the trees to ground level. Nguyen could smell the unfamiliar, acrid odor of the fumes as they permeated the atmosphere.

With a loud, violent crash—like that of a train wreck—the gigantic plane hit the mud flats and torturously skidded to a halt. The impact threw mud in all directions, momentarily concealing the plane from Nguyen's view. The plane landed near an island on which he had played as a child. The thunderous sound seemed to reverberate up and down the river for many seconds.

Not oblivious to the two bundles that had ejected and landed not far from him, Nguyen, eyes wide in amazement, was more awestruck by the sight of the American war machine that, like a comet from deep space, had come too close. He stared disbelievingly at the stationary plane, now in steaming ruins not more than four or five hundred meters from where he had been smoking his cigarette. The giant American plane, which had seemed invincible in the air just moments before, now sat lifeless, silent in the dark mud at the edge of the Song Ma.

Although the aircraft, still smoking, sat motionless, the mud seemed to be moving all around it. Nguyen soon realized that he was seeing mud crabs scurrying away in all directions from the impact of the alien, metal behemoth.

Nguyen heard loud shouting and screaming behind him. He turned to see the commotion of villagers running toward what he knew would be the American airmen. But, in continuing disbelief at what he had just witnessed, he turned back to stare at the *may bay my*. Nguyen realized that something extraordinary had just happened. He would never forget the approximate time of day or the day itself. The incident occurred mid-afternoon on Sunday, the 14th of May 1967.

Chapter 2
Thanh Hoa and Cau Ham Rong

VIETNAM, WITH ITS HEAD IN THE NORTH AND its long, crooked tail streaming south, is a narrow country that has been likened to a dragon, or perhaps a seahorse. Its entire eastern edge is bounded by the South China Sea and, to the north, more specifically, by the Gulf of Tonkin. Vietnam shares borders to the west with remote parts of Laos and Cambodia and to the north with China.

Northern Vietnam can be generally divided into three geographic strata: coastal flats with a sloping rise to the west to the jagged piedmonts, which rise further into sharp, angular, sheer limestone mountains with deep valleys and ravines. The precipitous mountains are the result of geologic uplift and tectonic action. It is from these mountains that the rivers rise to flow eastward to the sea. The northern land generally drains from northwest to southeast as the rivers empty into the Gulf of Tonkin.

Although much of Vietnam is covered with rugged, sometimes steep mountains, the Vietnamese, as they are known today, were not originally a mountain people per se. It's not known precisely from where their culture sprang but there is enough evidence to suggest that very early people lived in limestone caves along the northern rivers and may have come from various Australasian islands.

Vietnam is, historically, an agrarian country with rice being the primary crop for many hundreds of years. The country is host to two large river delta systems: the Mekong River in the south and the Red River in the north. Over the last many thousands of years, as the Chinese began to descend south into Vietnam, the culture evolved further. As a result, civilizations, benefiting from the rich soil deposited by the rivers over millions of years, flourished in the coastal regions. It was along the coastal plains, that the Vietnamese proliferated, jumping estuary by estuary, river by river, onto the soggy plains of southern Vietnam.

One such river, the Ma River—or Song Ma in Vietnamese—follows the typical drainage pattern, northwest to southeast. Beginning in the mountains of the western provinces, the Song Ma collects rain water from its drainage basin and its tributaries and carries it to its mouth, where the fresh, but muddy water from the river blends with the saltwater of the sea.

Nestled beside the Song Ma, many hundreds, or perhaps as long ago as a thousand years, the town of Thanh Hoa was founded. Located about a hundred fifty kilometers south of Hanoi, Thanh Hoa, now capital of the province of the same name, was once a small kingdom that grew into a commercial and agricultural center of some repute. Thanh Hoa boasts of several interesting features such as the Ba Trieu Temple, the Ho Dynasty Citadel, built from large blocks of green granite and, not far away, the Dao Grotto.

In the mid-1960s, remains of early human activity were discovered on a mountain in Thanh Hoa Province. Although subject to debate, the finds from that site have been dated as far back as 30,000 years. These artifacts may have been the result of the first settlement in Vietnam. Today, Thanh Hoa is best known for its porcelain and *nem*, a sort of sausage wrapped in banana leaves in the shape of a neat, tiny box. Thanh Hoa is bounded to the east by the flat plains that meet the sea and to the immediate west by a long, jagged, forested splinter of the Annamite Range.

Thanh Hoa is reached from Hanoi by *Quoc Luong* (National Highway) 1 or by a parallel narrow-gauge (one meter) railway. The two modes of transportation combined constitute the main north-south transportation artery connecting quaint, staid Hanoi in the north with busy, cosmopolitan Saigon (now Ho Chi Minh City) in the south. The road and railroad cross each of the eastward flowing rivers, sometimes in quick succession.

Beginning in Hanoi, the railroad originally reached only as far south as the tiny town of Vinh, which had an important port. The line south to Vinh was constructed in three sections: Hanoi to Nam Dinh, Nam Dinh to Thanh Hoa, and Thanh Hoa to Vinh. While the French Colonies Public Works Committee decreed construction was to begin on the Hanoi to Nam Dinh and Thanh Hoa to Vinh sections in 1899, initiation of construction for the middle link connecting Nam Dinh with Thanh Hoa would have to wait for a work decree to be issued one year later.

While rivers of lesser width were easily crossed, spanning the Song Ma presented a very different problem for French engineers. Railway alignment and geotechnical analysis of the area indicated that the only feasible place to cross the Song Ma was at a narrow isthmus a few kilometers northwest of Thanh Hoa near a small village located on the north side of the river.

Positioning of the bridge could be viewed as a study in engineering economics. Although the railway ran north-south, the bridge would cross the river in an almost due east-west direction. Construction of the bridge would take advantage of the geographical layout and it would be as short as possible.

Historically, three bridges were built at this location. French designers chose a special concept for the first bridge. Designed and constructed as a double steel arch with vertical steel members supporting the deck, the Song Ma was finally spanned in the 1930s. The arch was articulated or hinged at three points: at either end and in the middle. The apex of the bridge's arch rose twenty-five meters above the deck. The bridge crossed the Song Ma in one clear span of one hundred sixty-two meters and was ten meters wide. Serving primarily the railroad but with roadways for vehicles on each side, the structure was christened Cau Ham Rong; Ham Rong Bridge

The name Ham Rong was derived from two geologic formations, one each located on either bank of the river. Nui Rong, a sharp, jagged mountain, stands on the south (or west) side of the river and resembles a jawbone of a long mythological serpent whose body and tail were represented by the spiny mountain ridge that tapered southward. On the opposite bank, a small, elongated hillock referred to as Nui Ngoc (meaning "jade mountain"), the other jawbone, juts upward in solitary isolation. Both geologic features serve as silent sentinels protecting the narrow isthmus and the approaches to Cau Ham Rong, the name of which, when translated into English, literally means "dragon's jaw bridge."

Built with Vietnamese—some may argue, slave—labor, the elegance of Cau Ham Rong's sweeping steel arch and vertical steel stays compelled people from all over Southeast Asia to come to Thanh Hoa just to marvel at the bridge. To some, it was one of the most beautiful structures ever to adorn French Indochina.

Cau Ham Rong, the first bridge that dared to cross the Song Ma, quickly became the pride of Thanh Hoa. But to some Vietnamese who had developed more nationalistic leanings later on, Cau Ham Rong carried a more invidious implication: the bridge represented the repression exacted by the colonial rule of France. To deny the French use of their railway, and to compromise this symbol of colonial arrogance, the Vietminh—nationalist armed forces led by Ho Chi Minh—destroyed the bridge in 1945.

The second and third Ham Rong bridges, not as dramatic but held in no less esteem, were designed by a structural engineer from Hanoi named Nguyen Dinh Doan. Construction of a second Cau Ham Rong began in the 1950s and took many years to complete. It was this second bridge—of a more basic design than its predecessor—that, depending on one's point of view, became the most famous or infamous of all the bridges.

Simple steel bridges, the original, exotic steel-arched bridge of Cau Ham Rong notwithstanding, were commonly either of the longitudinal steel beam system with transverse supporting members, or a drive-through truss design, typical of the Warren truss developed in Britain and patented by James Warren in the mid-nineteenth century. The Warren truss gained rapid popularity and was exported throughout the world. But this bridge type was suitable for relatively short spans or for crossings where many supporting piers could be constructed. Recognizing relatively scarce material resources and the limitations of construction techniques that existed in Vietnam in the 1960s, Nguyen Dinh Doan reverted to the simple drive-through Warren steel truss to re-span the Song Ma.

In stark contrast to the original Cau Ham Rong, which spanned the river in an elegantly spectacular arch, the river crossing was beyond the structural capacity of a single Warren truss-type bridge. Two trusses would be required to span the river. One end of each Warren truss was supported on the opposite banks of the river by massive abutments. The free ends of each truss that met over the middle of the river were supported by a large oval-shaped concrete pier. The overall length of the bridge was one hundred sixty-five meters, not much longer than the original arch bridge.

The second Cau Ham Rong was dedicated personally by Ho Chi Minh on his birthday on 19 May 1964. To commemorate the second bridge's dedication, North Vietnam's Tien Bo Printing House issued to the public a postage stamp designed by Do Viet Tuan (pronounced, *zo vyet twan*), a well-known artist and illustrator of Vietnam's history. Printed in soft tri-colors, Cau Ham Rong, depicted in a tranquil setting, is seen obliquely from the north side looking east toward the small hillock called Nui Ngoc.

Cau Ham Rong, a dominant feature in an otherwise featureless area of Thanh Hoa Province, facilitated North Vietnam's military re-supply effort to South Vietnam and was, in general, an essential element of the north-south transportation network of North Vietnam.

Cau Ham Rong, the Ham Rong Bridge (which the Americans referred to as the Thanh Hoa Bridge), became a primary target of American military planners. The Americans tried to sever North Vietnam's capability to send men and war materiel south to Vinh and eventually farther south along the Ho Chi Minh Trail to South Vietnam. Perhaps an argument could be made that the Ham Rong Bridge had little strategic value, given that other bridges crossing other rivers could be more easily destroyed or that goods and material crossed the Song Ma by other means.

The bridge was the pride of the citizens of Thanh Hoa. If not considered the most famous bridge in North Vietnam, it became an icon for the North Vietnamese. The Ham Rong Bridge represented national pride and the symbol of resistance for the North Vietnamese. It rose in stature in the collective conscience of the country's citizenry. From the North Vietnamese perspective, the Ham Rong Bridge represented Ho Chi Minh, Vietnam, and the struggle against foreign intervention. Because of this symbolism, from the American perspective, destruction of the bridge may have become all the more important. Influenced by these ideas, it soon became incumbent on the antagonists on the one hand to obliterate it and on the other to protect it. While it was this second Ham Rong Bridge that the United States Government sought to destroy, it was this same bridge the Vietnamese vowed would never be destroyed.

Realizing the bridge's attractiveness to American military planners, the Vietnamese, using a sophisticated array of antiaircraft weaponry, passionately defended the pride of Thanh Hoa. Primarily because of the Ham Rong Bridge, Thanh Hoa found itself thrust into new historical circumstances and a new role at odds with the picturesque serenity of the province: fending off American attacks from the air and protecting its only bridge from destruction. Destruction of the second Ham Rong Bridge would eventually happen but only at great cost to both sides.

Nguyen Dinh Doan became famous for his design and re-construction of the Ham Rong Bridge. He received multiple accolades from his government.

At about the same time that Nguyen Dinh Doan was laboring with his concept and calculations in Thanh Hoa and Hanoi to design the second Ham Rong Bridge, half a world away in St. Louis, Missouri, another engineer was equally hard at work putting finishing touches on the design of a new military aircraft, the F-4 Phantom II.

Chapter 3
The Air War over North Vietnam

THE FRENCH INDOCHINA WAR, FOUGHT FROM about 1945 to 1954 between French colonial forces and Vietnamese revolutionaries, ended with a long, bloody siege at a large French military installation in the mountains west of Hanoi called Dien Bien Phu. The French Union's intent at Dien Bien Phu, had been to draw out Vietminh forces for a quick defeat, but embarrassing blunders led to the French Union's defeat instead.

General Vo Nguyen Giap (pronounced, *vo when jiap*), the architect of the siege of the French garrison, and his army of tens of thousands of Viet Minh soldiers hauling heavy artillery through narrow passes and up the sides of steep mountains completely surrounded the French. General Christian de Castries, overwhelmed, his troops badly mauled, finally surrendered to the Viet Minh.

After the fall of Dien Bien Phu, the Geneva Convention drew up the Geneva Accords, which called for France's withdrawal from Indochina and for a temporary demarcation between the communist Vietminh in northern Vietnam and those Vietnamese loyal to French rule in the south, until elections in 1956 could establish reunification. The demarcation occurred at the Ben Hai River or what was more commonly known, due to the river's approximate latitude, as the 17th Parallel.

America's loose, somewhat tacit involvement in the early sixties and its eventual investment in Vietnam resulted from the residual effects of the debacle at Dien Bien Phu and the subsequent partitioning of the country. Step by step, America became more deeply embroiled in a seething conflict from which there seemed little chance of withdrawal. The promised 1956 elections never materialized, and conflict only intensified for years afterward, eventually breaking into the Vietnam War, as it came to be called in America; or conversely, what the Vietnamese referred to as *Chien Tranh Chong My*, or, loosely translated, the American War.

The Vietnam War consisted of two distinct conflicts. First, there was the war in South Vietnam fought primarily on the ground with support from the air. This was often referred to as the ground war. The second conflict consisted of the aerial bombing campaigns, interdiction, air defense and dogfights over North Vietnam, collectively called the air war. As the Vietnam War escalated, so too did the air war escalate in a manner and to an extent some may feel was disproportionate to the size of the conflict.

As North Vietnam snubbed its nose at the might of America, it was this same might that America invoked to protect South Vietnam, tenuously allied to the United States and vulnerable to its aggressive northern neighbor. But quelling the North Vietnamese, who aligned with communist dogma and rhetoric and were supported by regimes in China and the Soviet Bloc countries, was not without its challenges.

To compromise North Vietnam's war-making capabilities and in an attempt to hammer it into submission, the United States, turning to its two major air arms, attacked the enemy from land bases and from the sea. This air war was conducted and fought solely by squadrons of the U.S. Air Force, U.S. Navy and U.S. Marine Corps, and opposed by various air defenses of the North Vietnamese.

The first American air loss in the escalating Southeast Asia conflict occurred over Laos in the spring of 1961 when a C-47 from Vientiane sustained enemy ground fire and crashed, killing its crew. The first recorded loss in Vietnam (north or south) occurred with the crash of a C-123 during a training flight in early February of 1962. The first combat loss occurred at the end of August 1962 when a T-28 was shot down south of Soc Trang in southern Vietnam. In all, ten propeller-driven aircraft were lost in Southeast Asia in 1962.

The air war escalated incrementally, insidiously. During the following year, 1963, American aircraft losses totaled about sixteen, many of which were C-123s, B-26s, T-28s; and two O-1s. These were all propeller-driven aircraft. No jet aircraft were lost in 1962 or 1963.

With its decision in the spring of 1964 to increase air support in Southeast Asia, the United States deployed in the intervening months and at different line periods, overall, four attack aircraft carriers to the south western Pacific. These included the USS *Ticonderoga* (CVA-14), USS *Bon Homme Richard* (CVA-31), USS *Constellation* (CVA-64) and the USS *Kitty Hawk* (CVA-63).

The USS *Kitty Hawk* was the first U.S. carrier to launch combat sorties in Southeast Asia (over Laos) and the first carrier to sustain the loss of an aircraft from her air wing. During the first week of June 1964, an RF-8 reconnaissance Crusader from *Kitty Hawk* was shot down over the Plain of Jars and became the first jet aircraft of the conflict to be shot down. The next day, an F-8, also from *Kitty Hawk*, was shot down over Laos as it escorted an RF-8 during a reconnaissance mission.

In response to what came to be called the Gulf of Tonkin Incident, involving American and much smaller North Vietnamese naval forces on 2 August 1964, F-8s from the USS *Ticonderoga* (one of which was flown by Charles Everett Southwick) responded to North Vietnam PT boat attacks on the USS *Maddox* (DD-731), a destroyer. This engagement may have been the first officially recorded combat mission by U.S. jet aircraft in North Vietnam.

It was on 5 August 1964, during a limited air operation called *Pierce Arrow*, that North Vietnamese land targets suffered the first major strike by U.S. aircraft launched from the USS *Ticonderoga* and USS *Constellation*. Navy strike aircraft from *Constellation* attacked the torpedo boat base at Hon Gay and another base at Loc Chao. Other launches originating from *Ticonderoga* struck bases at Quang Khe and Ben Thuy, and at the oil storage depot at Vinh. During these strikes the U.S. Navy lost two planes from *Constellation*: a propeller-driven A-1H Skyraider, its pilot killed, and an A-4C Skyhawk, its pilot, LTJG (Lieutenant Junior Grade) Everett Alvarez, captured.

Alvarez spent more than eight years in captivity, making him the second longest held American prisoner of war (POW) in U.S. history and the longest held in Hanoi. His A-4C was the first jet aircraft lost to combat over North Vietnam. On the same day, an F-8 from the USS *Bon Homme Richard* was lost during a training flight and a U.S. Air Force B-57B Canberra was lost due to bad weather and subsequent collision with another plane near Bien Hoa in South Vietnam.

By mid-August 1964, the U.S. Congress had passed the Gulf of Tonkin Resolution. As a result, American armed forces transitioned from an advisory role to one of more direct combat involvement. The American military buildup in Southeast Asia began in earnest.

The twin-engine B-57 Canberra bombers stationed at Bien Hoa near Saigon in 1964 were soon joined by tactical aircraft, namely the U.S. Air Force F-100 Super Sabre (America's first supersonic jet fighter). The tempo of the war was increasing.

Super Sabres had been operating from Thailand and South Vietnam on temporary rotation since 1962. The first F-100 Super Sabre was shot down over Laos in mid-August 1964. Although a very capable fighter and effective ground support aircraft, armed with four machine guns mounted just below the nose intake, the Super Sabre was phased out and replaced by the much larger F-105 Thunderchief.

"Thuds," as the F-105s were commonly called, began to arrive in Southeast Asia. The F-105s carried much of the brunt of the U.S. Air Force's combat activities against North Vietnam.

Pilots of the Thunderchiefs found themselves in an unfamiliar role since the Thunderchief was originally intended to be a quick-response weapon based primarily in Western Europe. It was developed as a super high-speed, low-level, air-to-ground delivery system of nuclear weapons, one of which was concealed in its enclosed bomb bay. With supersonic speed and stability at low levels, the Thunderchief was designed to penetrate the airspace of the Soviet Union and deliver its nuclear weapons with precision and with hopes that it could not be detected by the Russians until it was too late. For survival, the pilots relied on the lightning speed of the aircraft. One pilot observed, "*It couldn't turn very well but, my God, was it ever fast!*"

With combat resources from the U.S. Air Force and U.S. Navy now committed, the air war in Vietnam changed significantly.

U.S. Marines arrived in South Vietnam on the beaches of Da Nang. Military bases began to proliferate around the country. Due to the high exposure of aircraft to ground attack, the U.S. Air Force operated most of its aircraft from bases in Thailand.

Gargantuan eight-engine B-52 Stratofortress bombers were stationed at bases in Thailand, Guam, and the Philippines and began their famous "arc light" raids against concentrations of enemy forces in South Vietnam and Laos.

Eventually the U.S. Air Force deployed a special variable swept-wing, two-man fighter bomber, the F-111. Called the Aardvark, the F-111 was technologically advanced, but its sustained effectiveness proved questionable. After only about sixty missions and a few losses, the Aardvark was withdrawn from service in Southeast Asia for several years.

The Cobra helicopter gunship was developed for the U.S. Army to support ground troops. The Korean-vintage Skyraider, a very large, brutish, single-propeller-driven aircraft, became famous. It could stay on station over its target for a long time and deliver massive amounts of various ordnance. But the Skyraider's slow speed and low altitude missions made it vulnerable to ground fire.

The highly secret Blackbird flew high altitude aerial reconnaissance missions. Giant propeller-driven aircraft such as the Lockheed Constellation provided continuous airborne liaison and airspace control to all American air combatants. Converted Boeing 707s flew air-refueling missions.

Aging DC-3s and the four-engine C-130 Hercules turboprop aircraft were converted into gun ships. Protruding from the left (or port) side of the fuselage, the machine guns mounted in these modified planes could fire ammunition at astonishing rates. Their rate of fire was so fast that no single detonation could be discerned. It was an uninterrupted, continuous, clamoring chain of sound.

Douglas Aircraft Company's DC-8s and Boeing's 707s, operated by private air transport companies, flew into and out of South Vietnam from the United States. In Vietnam and elsewhere in Southeast Asia, Air America and Continental Airlines had their own fleets of strange aircraft operating nefariously under the auspices of the U.S. Central Intelligence Agency (CIA).

Not nearly as colorful as the names given each aircraft, the list of planes by their alphanumeric designations highlighted the extent to which America eventually committed its military air resources during the conflict. In an impressive pantheon of American military aviation, America's air armada, to identify some in no particular order, included the F-105, F-100, F-111, A-6, A-7, A-3, EB-66, B-26, B-57, B-52, F-5, A-1, T-34, F-101, F-102, F-106, RF-8, SR-71, OV-1, O-1, O-2, OV-10, C-47, AC-47, EC-47, U-2, C-117, C-123, C-119, C-123, CV-2, C-130, EC-121, KC-135, C-118, C-124, C-141, DC-9, C-5A, OH-6, UH-1, CH-46, CH-47, and the giant CH-53 helicopter and its cousin, the CH-54 Sky Crane.

Continuing with an operational blueprint that began in 1964 and which would be followed to varying degrees for the next nine years, America's aircraft carriers with sixty to eighty aircraft embarked on each were continuously sent to the Gulf of Tonkin. While two or perhaps three attack carriers operated simultaneously in the Gulf, as many as five carriers would operate or be in transition to or from the coast of Vietnam at any one time. Carriers rotated on and off line every few weeks. While on line, the carriers shared the day, operating in twelve hour shifts, midnight to noon and from noon to midnight. The Gulf of Tonkin, not being a particularly large geographical area in which to operate large aircraft carriers and with the carrier forces stationed as they were, the planes would, within minutes, transition from the safety of the sea to the hostilities that awaited them in the world's most heavily defended area: North Vietnam.

The U.S. Navy deployed single-engine attack bombers, the tiny A-4 Sky-hawk and the larger A-7 Corsair, and the twin-engine A-3 Skywarrior. The Navy also used an awesome attack plane called the A-6 Intruder. The dual-engine Intruder, for its size, could carry a staggering number of bombs. The A-6 caused considerable damage to North Vietnam. The Navy used the RA-5C and RF-8 for reconnaissance. For fighters, it used the coveted F-8 Crusader.

An unorthodox plane with a strange profile or appearance arrived on the scene in great numbers: the F-4 Phantom II. The F-4 may have been the most prolific combat fixed-wing aircraft during the entire Vietnam conflict. As the B-17, B-29, P-51, P-38, ME-109, or the Japanese Zero came to characterize World War II; or the F-86 and MiG-15 the Korean conflict; along with the Huey helicopter, the B-52, and the M-16 and AK-47 opposing automatic assault weapons, the F-4, with its enigmatic name, would come to symbolize to many the war in Vietnam. Even though the F-105 and A-6 carried much of the burden of the bombing campaign along with the overpowering bombing capabilities of the B-52, it is the F-4 that will most probably be associated with the Vietnam War.

Operational statistics began to accumulate rapidly, eventually to overwhelm. During 1964, about sixty U.S. aircraft had been lost in Southeast Asia, almost four times the number lost in 1963. During 1965, the United States lost about three hundred eighty aircraft in Southeast Asia—six times the number lost the previous year. The air war grew to unbelievable proportions, an oft quoted statistic being that more than twice as many bombs were dropped in Vietnam than were released during all of World War II. There were reports that due to the high rate of expenditure of bombs in Vietnam, many missions were flown with partial loads to keep the sortie rate up, a statistic that was important to some in Washington, D.C.

America's awesome air power figured largely in strategic plans developed by General William C. Westmoreland to win the Vietnam War decisively. About halfway through the war, in 1967 and early 1968, as a result of high-level planning, General Westmoreland attempted to taunt the North Vietnamese communists with more than seven thousand U.S. Marines under the command of Marine Colonel David E. Lownds at a remote outpost on Highway Nine called Khe Sanh. Westmoreland hoped to draw out the opposing forces under Brigadier General Tran Quy Hai, who reported to General Vo Nguyen Giap, into an all-out attack against the beleaguered U.S. Marine base located in the deceptively soft, scenic hills just south of the DMZ (demilitarized zone or the 17th parallel) in Quang Tri Province. Colonel Lownds would summon the U.S. Air Force's giant B-52s to annihilate the enemy, thereby dealing the North Vietnamese Army a final, fatal blow. While Marines at the Khe Sanh Combat Base or those occupying various surrounding hills such as Hill 861 or Hill 881 were under a continuous rocket and artillery siege for almost eighty days, in what became known as the Battle of Khe Sanh, the all-out attack by the People's Army of Vietnam (PAVN), or more simply, NVA, and their planned subsequent destruction by U.S. bombing never happened.

Conducting the air war from the sea, the U. S. Navy's Seventh Fleet was hard-pressed to accomplish its mission without additional resources. Carriers from the U.S. Atlantic Fleet were ordered into the area. These carriers were required to make the long journey from the East Coast down around either Cape Horn (southern tip of South America) or the Cape of Good Hope (southern tip of Africa) to the Pacific Ocean. The carriers were too large to pass through the locks of the Panama Canal.

Yankee Station was the name given to that loose geographical region of the Gulf of Tonkin (generally above the 18th parallel) in which the carriers operated. Yankee Station was the final destination of a WestPac cruise. In the late sixties and early seventies, if a person was on a WestPac cruise, most certainly it meant he was on his way to Vietnam.

The air war over North Vietnam was fought in stages and, like the gridiron of a football field, by lines of latitude. Unlike lines of longitude, which converge at the poles, lines of latitude are parallel; they do not converge. Latitude and parallel became interchangeable expressions. While North and South Vietnam were separated at the 17th parallel, bombing "halts," or limits, were defined by other parallels farther north. One such bombing limitation was defined by the 20th parallel. That is, U.S. air strikes were prohibited above this latitude. But perhaps because the city of Thanh Hoa was below this parallel and so much damage was being inflicted on it, the bombing limits were moved farther south to the 19th parallel, thereby providing a theoretical shield to the city.

North Vietnam used its famed Ho Chi Minh Trail to run supplies south. The Ho Chi Minh Trail began in Vinh, trailed south, then west into Laos, and eventually slipped back east into South Vietnam. The flow of men and material south along the Ho Chi Minh Trail was interrupted, at times severely, by intense aerial bombing but it was never stopped. By the end of the war, so confident of their abilities, the North Vietnamese had constructed a six-inch fuel line from Vinh, near the Gulf of Tonkin in North Vietnam, almost to Pleiku, in the Central Highlands area of South Vietnam, a distance of a little over three hundred fifty miles.

The United States divided North Vietnam into bombing, or operational zones that were called route packages. Route package numbers started in the southern part of North Vietnam, with Route Package I (RP-I) being the farthest south. Risk to pilots rose proportionately as the route packages increased in numerical designation. Route Package VI was most dangerous as it included the Hanoi and Haiphong areas. RP-VI was further divided into VIa and VIb, which were demarked by a north-south railway that divided Hanoi. Although from time to time there was some cross-over, the Air Force was given RP-VIa while the Navy was confined to RP-VIb.

Operation Rolling Thunder, a U.S. bombing campaign, was implemented to increase pressure on Hanoi to cease hostilities. The campaign moved north on an incremental basis, with the intention of strangling North Vietnam's infrastructure and restricting its movement. The government of North Vietnam became convinced that Hanoi would soon become the ultimate target. North Vietnam's resolve hardened, their leadership became more recalcitrant.

Bombing may have forestalled or frustrated the war-making capabilities of North Vietnam, but the military policies implemented by the U.S. government did not win the Vietnam War for America. The B-52 raids against targets around Hanoi and Haiphong, late in the war, forced negotiations that subsequently ended the war, but the intervening bombing throughout the war did not stop North Vietnam's military actions.

Although the ground war in South Vietnam would not reach its zenith until 1968, if one was a naval or air force aviator and survived 1967, statistically speaking, chances were that one would survive the war. With more than six hundred aircraft lost in 1967, not counting the twenty-two planes destroyed during a major fire aboard the USS *Forrestal* (CVA-59), more U.S. fixed-wing aircraft were downed in that year than during any other year of the conflict.

Chapter 4
The Air Defense of North Vietnam

NORTH VIETNAM'S RAPID DEVELOPMENT OF AN effective air defense system to ward off the high-tech sophistication of the U.S. military was a remarkable evolution. When the war began, it seemed unlikely that North Vietnam could employ the resources to man and manage sophisticated, technologically advanced air defense systems beyond simple load-aim-shoot antiaircraft artillery (AAA), or "Triple-A" as it came to be called. It soon became apparent, however, that Hanoi was resourceful. The North Vietnamese resorted to other means and would astonish the world in a relatively short time.

With the assistance of the Soviet Union and Soviet Bloc countries and through a thorny relationship with China, a country with whom Vietnam maintained fragile relations, North Vietnamese military air defense planners came to rely on a steady influx of materiel, enhanced equipment, radars, MiG aircraft, and, perhaps the most lethal threat of all, surface-to-air missiles, or SAMs. North Vietnam became a formidable air defense fortress that could be characterized as a triad of interrelated and to some degree interdependent systems that included ground-based weapons, SAMs, and fighter aircraft.

What the Vietnamese called the "American War," Ho Chi Minh, himself, called the "People's War" because for example, in its most elemental state, North Vietnam's air defense system found its simplified origins in its people—through its men and women wielding old rifles and carbines and shoulder-held automatic weapons.

The defense ministry produced aircraft identification manuals for its citizens that depicted, with fair accuracy, various types of U.S. aircraft. People were given guidance as to how to identify combat aircraft, including elementary knowledge of their mission capabilities and flight characteristics. Classes providing instruction to the common person as to how to harass attacking aircraft with their small-caliber weapons were held in the neighbor-hoods and districts of Hanoi and Haiphong, and in smaller cities, towns, and villages throughout the country. The Vietnamese devised wood and pa-pier-mâché models that imitated the silhouettes of American planes. These were placed on tight strings and pulled at various angles and speeds. The size and speed of the models and their distances from the observer mimic-ked planes at various angles, low altitudes, and distances. People practiced their aiming skills by sighting on the models as they were pulled along the string. They were taught how to "lead" a moving aircraft in the same man-ner that a waterfowl hunter might lead a flying duck.

Many Vietnamese soon became proficient at identifying U.S. aircraft by type, name, and number designation. The rooftops in Hanoi and Haiphong were populated with men and women who sported rifles and old machine guns and kept a skyward vigil. Individually-armed citizens were not a major threat to U.S. aircraft. The image of a woman pointing her ancient carbine skyward juxtaposed against the sophistication of American air weaponry may seem comical. Collectively, however, this citizens' air defense force proved effective and dangerous to American airmen.

Of course, the North Vietnamese air defense employed more modern weaponry, with the machine gun figuring highly into the overall air defense system. The Soviet-made ZPU-44—a compact, multi-barreled 14.5mm (.50-caliber) machine gun—proved especially deadly because of the high rate of sustained fire from its multiple barrels. Easy to disassemble and reassemble and conceal, the ZPU-44 was very mobile and was often placed on rooftops.

The use of Chinese- and Soviet-made antiaircraft cannons bolstered the first element of the air defense triad. In its single or double-barrel variant, the 37mm antiaircraft gun was perhaps the least sophisticated but the easi-est to deploy and use. It was highly mobile and very reliable. Munitions were easy to handle, and the gun could be concealed and repositioned easily. The 37mm had a range of about three miles. It had the capability of hitting planes effectively at altitudes up to 6,000 feet with a relatively high rate of success. Its explosive warhead was comparable to the charge in a hand grenade. Numbering more than ten thousand throughout North Vietnam, the 37mm antiaircraft cannon proved effective and became a building block on which North Vietnam's air defense system was conceived.

In addition to the 37mm cannon, the North Vietnamese used other anti-aircraft artillery that ranged from 57mm to the much larger-bore 85mm,

100mm, 110mm and 120mm guns. Some of these guns ironically were American-made left over from World War II and supplied by East Germany and the Soviet Union. Some of the larger-bore Soviet guns, the projectiles from which could reach high altitudes, were radar-controlled. Electronic countermeasures and radar-seeking munitions, however, often rendered them ineffective.

In general—there never was a hard and fast rule—the larger the bore of the weapon, the farther it was placed from what the North Vietnamese would perceive as a primary target for the Americans. The 110mm and 120mm guns, for example, were of a more strategic value and, due to the higher altitude of the projectile's apogee, they ringed Hanoi and Haiphong and were sometimes placed near the coast. The 57mms were placed closer to potential targets and tightened the circle of fire on American planes as they dove to strike their targets. Because of their faster rate of fire and reduced range, the smaller-caliber 37mm antiaircraft artillery units and the 14.5mm ZPU-44s or larger 23mm cannons were placed very near to potential targets, such as bridges, as the last line of defense against attacking aircraft.

Each antiaircraft gun had its signature effect. Airbursts from 57mm guns were black and those from 37mm guns were white. The larger guns fired at slower rates. Loaded from the side, the 57mm's sound was characterized by regular but intermittent reports: boom ... boom ... boom ... boom—four shots at a time. The 37mms, their ammunition fed into the breach vertically (downward), were a little faster: boom, boom, boom, boom, boom. The 14.5mm and 23mms sounded like the machine guns that they were.

The second element of the air defense triad was surface-to-air missiles. SAMs came in a variety of designations but most prominent were the SAM II and the more effective, longer range SAM III. SAMs were basically of a two-stage design: the first, the booster stage, provided the power for a fast liftoff and then fell away seconds later as the second stage ignited and accelerated the missile to its target. SAMs were placed all around Hanoi and Haiphong but usually were ten to twenty kilometers from any target. The SAM bases themselves became targets for the Americans and were defended by the smaller-caliber artillery units.

SAMs were stored in a sundry of places including at times in neighborhoods, inside long but narrow shops along the main streets of Hanoi and Haiphong and throughout the villages. In Hanoi during the height of the air war, an unending parade of transporters carrying SAMs could sometimes be seen as the missiles were transported at night from downtown Hanoi to the launch sites.

Finally, the MiG jet fighter represented the third element of North Vietnam's air defense system. North Vietnam used Soviet- and Chinese-made MiGs. A few Vietnamese pilots became relatively skilled and adroit foes of U.S. aircraft. It's conceivable—in fact, evidently a few reports are beginning to emerge—that Soviet and maybe Chinese pilots flew some, perhaps many, of the missions.

Curiously, the first Ace of the Vietnam War was not an American. He was a North Vietnamese pilot named Nguyen Van Bai (pronounced, *when van by*). But eventually America would have its Aces—pilots who had shot down at least five enemy aircraft. Navy pilot Randy Cunningham, accompanied in the back seat of his F-4 by Willie Driscoll, his radar intercept officer (RIO), Air Force pilot Steve Richie, with Charles Debellevue sitting behind him as the weapons systems officer (WSO), in their F-4, and Jeff Feinstein, an Air Force weapons systems officer, would become the only American Aces of the war. Debellevue, not reaching Ace status while flying with Richie, would eventually become the highest-scoring American Ace, with a total of six kills. While North Vietnam could boast of the first Ace and—they claim—about three times more Aces than the United States, the reality was they didn't have better pilots, they just had more targets.

North Vietnam's antiaircraft artillery and SAM systems were not static. They were deployed, moved, removed, moved around, concealed, repositioned, and moved again. MiG aircraft were hidden in caves, beneath trees, and even among houses in villages. The North Vietnamese resorted to making decoys of various ground-to-air weapons. A cadre of craftsmen was dedicated to fabricating phony antiaircraft artillery and SAMs and their emplacements in an attempt to fool and frustrate American pilots and attack planners who tried to keep continuous tabs on the locations of North Vietnam's air defenses.

Hanoi depended on three systems of alert. First, radar was very important to Hanoi because of its early warning and ground control capability. The Soviet Fan Song radar was most effective. Radar had long eyes but was easily detected and compromised by radar-seeking missiles.

Second, relying again on human resources, observers stood as lookouts in camouflaged towers that lined the eastern coast and the mountains to the west. Upon sighting the approaching enemy they would telephone Hanoi, where central control of the air defense system was maintained. As a backup, villagers would also ring bells or gongs—some made from the shells of unexploded bombs. Others would pick up the signal and ring another bell or gong. In this way, as the planes moved closer to their targets, the gongs would provide a secondary warning as their sound, relayed again and again, moved quickly west from the coast or east from the mountains. The North Vietnamese developed their own special code of alert. A type of bell or an arrangement of sound would indicate the size of the striking force, type of aircraft, and apparent direction and altitude.

There was a third, less precise system: spies. Launches from U.S. aircraft carriers were sometimes monitored by Soviet trawlers who would relay launch time and strength and type of aircraft to the North Vietnamese. This may also have happened in Thailand and elsewhere. Reports were that observers sympathetic to North Vietnam watched American planes taking off from bases in Thailand or the Philippines and relayed this information to Hanoi.

Chapter 5

Beyond America: The Extension of Power (Task Force 77, CVA-63, CVW-11 and VF-114)

AMERICAN CARRIER AVIATION BEGAN SHORTLY after World War I with the U.S. Navy's USS *Langley* (CV-1) serving as the first aircraft carrier in 1922. Since then, of course, both carrier aviation and aircraft carriers themselves have undergone enormous transformation. The aircraft carrier became the dominant vessel of U.S. naval might in World War II. It rendered the battleship, heretofore king of the seas, to a subordinate role. That turning point most likely came at the Battle of Midway, fought off Midway Island just west of Hawaii in June 1942, where, as a result of America's strategic use of aircraft carriers, the Japanese lost their opportunity to control the entire Pacific.

In May 1941, a year before the Battle of Midway, the British aircraft carrier, HMS *Ark Royal* played an important role in the sinking of the *Bismarck* (Germany's largest battleship), in the Atlantic. Torpedo-laden Fairey Swordfish biplanes from the *Ark Royal* severely damaged the *Bismarck* southwest of Ireland. This allowed other British warships to interdict and sink her. The action against the *Bismarck* in the Atlantic, and the Battle of Midway in the Pacific a year later, foretold the importance and future of naval aviation. The aircraft carrier has maintained its pre-eminent role as a war vessel ever since.

Some may argue that development of the nuclear submarine with its load of nuclear missiles held more strategic importance, for example, in deterring the USSR from attacking the United States. Although the silent, seemingly dormant, destructive capability of America's submarines cannot be questioned, it is, however, the carriers that respond with conspicuous swiftness and flexibility of mission. United States presidents have come to rely heavily on the carrier force and its obvious extension of power. America's aircraft carriers are able to react to any crisis almost anywhere in the world. They have been seen as a crucial element of America's ability to respond to ominous international military and humanitarian events.

As a result of popular Hollywood films but without an understanding of the composition or dichotomy of a carrier organization, understandably the general public may be left with the image of a carrier acting as a singular military entity. The representation may come across as that of a very large, "solely unique" organization that goes to sea to defend America or to deter adverse situations or which attacks the enemy from the air.

Forgetting the mind-boggling complexities of an aircraft carrier and its complicated systems, basically its operations consist of two distinct elements. The first element, the ship and her complement of many hundreds of sailors, provide the seagoing support platform for the second component, the air wing. Though under separate commands, an organizational relationship connects the two. This connection is found most obviously on the flight deck. But there are many functions of liaison, crossover, and close coordination between the two entities that may blur the distinction. For example, ordnance is delivered to the flight deck by the ship's company but it is attached to the planes and made ready by air wing personnel. Maintenance of the aircraft is performed by crew of the air wing. The men who direct planes to the catapults, as well as the catapult officers (who themselves are naval aviators) belong to the ship's company. On the receiving end or at recovery, the landing signal officers (also naval aviators)—those who stand at the stern of the carrier and bring the aircraft aboard the ship—belong to the squadrons, therefore the air wing. The crewmen who manage the planes to their stations once the aircraft is released from the arresting cable are again ship's company. Because of the interrelationship that exists between the ship and the air wing, every flying-related officer's billet (position) in the ship's company is filled with a naval aviator or a naval flight officer. Although the ship's captain belongs to the ship and not the air wing, he is also a naval aviator or a naval flight officer.

Without the air wing, the carrier may as well never leave port. Without the carrier, the air wing cannot project its power very far from U.S. shores and may as well become part of the U.S. Air Force. But many of the ship's crew know little about flying operations and many members of the air wing are not familiar with the inner workings of a ship, especially a carrier. Neither the ship's crew nor the air wing can receive sufficient training in the other discipline, so to speak, to fulfill the rigorous demands both of a carrier's operations and flying; hence, the necessary dichotomy. When converged, the two elements work together to provide operational synergy that complements each other and which makes the carrier the most daunting of military systems and a most impressive organizational structure.

A carrier is usually at sea for about eight consecutive months per cruise and, of those eight months, on line for about six months. She will set sail from her home port with her own crew and the crew of her own air wing. Although it has happened that some aircraft may join the carrier after it has left port, usually the aircraft are craned aboard prior to setting sail.

A total of twenty-one aircraft carriers operated in the waters off Vietnam during the Vietnam War, making, in the aggregate, eighty-six total deployments to the Tonkin Gulf. The oldest carrier was the USS *Yorktown* (CVS-10) and the youngest the USS *America* (CVA-66). Only one nuclear-powered carrier operated at that time in Vietnam's waters, the USS *Enterprise* (CVAN-65).

Some carriers made only one WestPac cruise while others made many. It was those carriers based on the western shores of the United States that bore the burden of the missions to the Tonkin Gulf and upon which the Seventh Fleet's Task Force 77 relied. Although Task Force 77's operations spanned a large part of the Far East, Task Force 77 was best known as the military designation of ships and crews that took part in combat operations in the waters off Vietnam.

While understanding the tangible presence of a ship or an airplane, appreciating their alphanumeric designations is not so easy. The goupings of letters "CVA," "CVW" and "VF" have evolved over many decades but have one thing in common: they each refer to flight related activities, as denoted by the letter "V." The origin of the use of V as a designator has been debated but it is generally thought to have been derived from the French verb *voler* (to fly), or simply from *vol* which means flight.

The USS *Kitty Hawk* bore the alphanumeric designation CVA-63 (Attack Carrier). Aircraft carriers came to be denoted by a "C," which is coincidental with the first letter of the word carrier but which originated from the same designation as that for cruisers. However, the second letter, "V," differentiates carriers from cruisers that might carry a two-letter designation such as CA, CB, CC, CL, or CS—stopping short of CV. To differentiate between types of carriers, a third letter was used such as CVB for large aircraft carrier, CVE for escort carrier, or CVL for light carrier. CVA simply meant attack aircraft carrier. CVA morphed in the mid 1970s to CV. Carriers were consecutively numbered (currently 1 through 77), regardless of carrier type.

On *Kitty Hawk* (and on all carriers), the second part of the identification tag, the number, clearly visible by its heroic size, is seen on three distinct locations on the ship: on the bow of the flight deck and on each side of the "island," the tall, multi-story super-structure towering above the flight deck on the starboard side of the ship that contains the navigation bridge and command center for flight deck operations.

USS *Kitty Hawk*, the first operational carrier of its class of the same name, began life in late 1956 when it was laid down by the New York Shipbuilding Corporation in the Camden, New Jersey shipyards. *Kitty Hawk* is 325 meters (1,065 feet) long and, at its widest extremity, 86 meters (282 feet) wide; it displaces 60,000 tons of water. Powered by eight steam boilers and four propellers, each twenty-one feet in diameter, she can attain a top speed of between thirty and thirty-five knots. One knot is one nautical mile per hour. A nautical mile, at 6,076 feet, is 796 feet longer than a statute mile. Thirty-five knots is roughly equal to forty miles per hour.

Other carriers in the *Kitty Hawk* class included the USS *Constellation*, (CVA-64; 1961-2003); USS *America*, (CVA-66; 1965-1996); and USS *John F. Kennedy*, (CVA-67; 1967-2007). The USS *Enterprise*, (CVAN-65; still operating), was constructed using the same structural layout as the other *Kitty Hawk* class carriers but because of its nuclear power plant it received a special designation.

Because of its size, operational statistics for *Kitty Hawk* (or any carrier for that matter) are impressive. Briefly, 12,000 to 15,000 meals are prepared daily; she carries two million gallons of fuel; potable water demand is met by distilling 340,000 gallons of sea water daily; the capacity of each aircraft elevator is 130,000 pounds. Many more statistics exist that attest to the extraordinary size and operations of the carrier.

Commissioned at the end of April 1961, the USS *Kitty Hawk* joined the Seventh Fleet in October 1962 and replaced the USS *Midway* (CVA-41) as the flagship. *Kitty Hawk* was host to important groups of dignitaries and distinguished visitors throughout her many years of service, not the least of whom included Bob Hope, Bob Considine, Barry Goldwater, Hedley Donovan (editor-in-chief of Time magazine), William Buckley, Dr. Billy Graham, Harry Bird, Henry Fonda, John Steinbeck, and President John F. Kennedy. In all, after the Gulf of Tonkin incident, between 1965 and the end of 1972, *Kitty Hawk* made six cruises to the Tonkin Gulf to conduct military operations against North Vietnam.

Fixed-wing aircraft were launched from *Kitty Hawk* through the operation of two bow catapults and two waist catapults, the length of which for each is about two hundred fifty feet. The waist catapults operated from the angled deck, which was also used for landing or, as the expression goes, recovery of returning aircraft.

Each carrier transported her own air wing with its own unique alphanumeric identification tag. The history of air wing designations is more complicated than that for carrier designations. In the early days of naval aviation, the assemblage of aircraft embarked on a carrier assumed the title of Air Group. More precisely, carrier air groups were originally identified only by the carrier's name such as the "Yorktown Air Group." The aircraft tails of the squadrons were color coded. Activated in 1937, "Carrier Air Group" was the original official description of the collection of aircraft on a carrier. Color coding was standardized not by squadrons but by carrier. The tails of the planes of the Yorktown Carrier Air Group were color coded with red, those of the Ranger Carrier Air Group green. Numerical designation of air groups such as CVG-5 or CVG-6 began in 1942 and replaced the informal reference to the carrier's name. There was no correlation between the assigned Air Group number and the number of the carrier. CVG-2 was assigned to (the first) USS *Enterprise* (CV-6), for example. Often referred to as CAG, the obvious acronym for carrier air group, officially the correct designation was CVG (again with use of the V). CAG in fact stood for "Commander of the Air Group" and the most senior ranking officer of the air group. He was expected to personally lead all major strike operations. In 1942, the identification system changed again.

The number of each air group corresponded to the hull number of the aircraft carrier. Hence CVG-2 was assigned to aircraft carrier CV-2, the USS *Lexington*. In mid-1944, the designations changed and a new set of letters was used to denote heavy, medium, light, and escort carrier air groups (CVBG, CVG, CVLG, CVEG) to more closely associate a type of air group with a type of carrier (CVL, CVB, or CVE). In 1948, all carrier air groups were re-designated simply as CVG. Finally, in 1963, Carrier Air Group became Carrier Air Wing and CVG became CVW.

Kitty Hawk was the seagoing home for Air Wing Eleven (CVW-11) during its involvement in the war in Vietnam. When *Kitty Hawk* sailed for Vietnam, Air Wing Eleven was embarked each time for cruise after cruise. During the Vietnam War an air wing consisted usually of two fighter squadrons and three attack squadrons and various other aircraft including helicopters assigned or attached to the air wing.

Squadrons within the air wings were denoted by as many as three letters. The evolution of this identification system is equally intricate. Briefly, in the very early days of naval aviation, navy planes were mostly stationed at land bases near the coast. But when more and more planes moved to carriers, squadron designations became imperative. Squadron designations identified the role of the aircraft in the squadron in much the same way that ships were identified. In 1920, squadrons were identified by two or more letters beginning with Z or V. The letter "Z," which may have been derived from Zeppelin, was reserved for balloons or dirigibles. The letter "V" denoted fixed-wing aircraft. The second and third letters after Z or V denoted function or the mission of a particular type of squadron. The letter "B" was reserved for bombing, later changed to "A" for attack (e.g., VA-144), and "F" stood for fighter squadrons (e.g., VF-114).

Air Wing Eleven was comprised of fighters, attack aircraft, reconnaissance planes, and refueling planes. Rotor craft (helicopters) worked in conjunction with the air wing but were part of the carrier's operations. There were usually at least two helicopters on *Kitty Hawk*.

Once aboard *Kitty Hawk*, during its 1966-67 cruise, the squadrons of Air Wing Eleven included two F-4 Phantom II fighter squadrons, VF-114 (Aardvarks) and VF-213 (Black Lions); three bomber, or attack squadrons, VA-112 (Bombing Broncos) and VA-144 (Roadrunners), both of which operated A-4 Skyhawks; and VA-85 (Black Falcons), which flew the A-6 Intruder. Further, an additional assortment of other fixed-wing aircraft, most notably A-3 Skywarriors and RA-5C Vigilantes, were detachments from their home squadrons and were assigned to CVW-11.

Storage area on *Kitty Hawk*, when devoid of anything in its capacious hangar deck and on its sprawling four-and-a-half-acre flight deck, may seem vast. At sea, however, being the repository of between seventy and eighty aircraft, *Kitty Hawk* was congested. Regardless of how huge an aircraft carrier may appear relative to a person's physical perspective, once it is crowded with large, hulking aircraft, space is at a premium.

It may seem, to some degree, that the role of one type of fixed-wing aircraft could fulfill the role of another type of fixed-wing aircraft, but practically speaking this did not happen to any real extent. There was not a lot of cross-over. While it was true that the F-4 and F-8 (Crusader) could carry bombs and make bomb runs, which they did, in addition to their role of fleet and carrier air defense, the reverse cannot necessarily be said of the attack planes. The A-3s, A-4s, A-6s and A-7s were the workhorses of the attack arm and primarily carried out bombing and rocket attacks. Reconnaissance was left to the RF-8 Crusaders and RA-5C Vigilantes.

As for VF-114 and VF-213, the two F-4 squadrons on *Kitty Hawk*, each squadron had as many as fourteen aircraft but usually deployed about ten on the ship, leaving the remainder behind for repair or replacement. While it makes sense to have a reserve, it is probably more likely that there was not enough room on the ship for the additional aircraft. This was particularly true with limited availability of maintenance space in the hangar deck. Most major aircraft maintenance was performed at land bases.

Each squadron had a squadron commander and, both individually and collectively, the squadron commanders reported to the air wing commander, referred to as CAG. The acronym is a holdover from a time long past when the air wing was referred to as the Carrier Air Group. The initials have been retained as a legacy title.

Although the squadron designation changed and morphed since its inception in 1945, fighter squadron VF-114 earned its current alphanumeric designation in 1950. The men called themselves "The Executioners." In 1961, they changed their name to the "Aardvarks" (not to be confused with the USAF F-111 variable swept-wing aircraft dubbed the Aardvark) and adopted the anteater character found in Johnny Hart's then-popular daily cartoon, "B.C." Other than the squadron number on each side of the fuselage, VF-114, during the 1966-67 cruise, displayed no brazen or daring markings on its aircraft except for an orange horizontal stripe at the top of the vertical stabilizer with a profile, a perfect likeness of Johnny Hart's anteater, inset in white.

Over the many years of VF-114's existence, its pilots flew a variety of aircraft including the F-6F Hellcat and F-4U4 Corsair, and then jets with the advent of the F-9F Panther, the F-2H Banshee, and the F-3H Demon.

VF-114 transitioned to the F-4 in 1961 and held the distinction of being the first Pacific fleet squadron to be armed with the latest combat aircraft. VF-114, always flying off *Kitty Hawk*, flew thousands of combat missions during the Vietnam War but produced no navy "Ace," as did VF-96 (Randy Cunningham and Willie Driscoll in an F-4) from *Constellation*. But pilots of

VF-114 shot down quite a few enemy aircraft in combat. To mark the victories of the entire air wing, the silhouettes of each enemy plane shot down are painted in red high up on the starboard side of *Kitty Hawk*'s island and can be seen still to this day. Those shot down by VF-114 are among them.

Chapter 6
The F-4 Phantom II

"TWO CREWMEN. TWO ENGINES. MACH 2 SPEED. Three-hour flight time." These were the instructions that aircraft designer Herman D. Barkey heard from a U.S. Navy contracting officer as the officer scrawled them on a blackboard sometime in late 1953. Having been ushered into a quiet, secure room at the large manufacturing facilities of McDonnell Aircraft Company in St. Louis, Barkey learned the Navy's latest defining design parameters from which a new U.S. Navy aircraft would emerge.

McDonnell had lost a previous competition to build a new carrier-based aircraft. The F-8 Crusader built by Chance Vought had won the competition and had been selected by the Navy. McDonnell was determined to stay in the aircraft business and to continue to design planes for aircraft carriers. Reeling from this latest contract loss, McDonnell dug its heels in. Under orders from James S. McDonnell, the company president, McDonnell engineers interviewed everyone from the Chief of Naval Operations (CNO) and personnel in the Bureau of Aeronautics down to any person who had an opinion of what the Navy wanted in an aircraft. As a result of this research, McDonnell set about designing a new aircraft. They made a mock-up and solicited comments and critiques from the Navy and sent invitations to high-ranking Navy personnel to come to St. Louis to see the mock-up and discuss the plane. The only problem facing McDonnell was that the Navy, at that time, had no requirement for the aircraft. McDonnell was taking a big risk with its investment in this venture. McDonnell's efforts could result in nothing. James McDonnell was tenacious, if not persistent, and marketed the Navy heavily. Not only did he want to build the plane, he was determined to continue the company's tradition and to keep his people employed. He hated the prospect of a lay-off. In November 1954, McDonnell received a letter of intent to design and manufacture two airplanes. The Navy had become interested in the fledgling project.

As with all aircraft designs, it's impossible to know early on where the criteria and parameters, component sizes, and design changes will lead the designer and what the ultimate product will look like. There is a lot of give and take. A person may have an idea of what the plane's role and its capabilities may or should be, but until the aircraft design begins to take shape on the drawing board and goes through countless tests, it is impossible to know what physical shape the aircraft will ultimately assume. Design teething is arduous, at times painful.

The original concept of the new aircraft included a single airman and two engines. Its top speed would be about one-and-a-half times the speed of sound.

"*And no guns.*"

"*What?*" Had Herman Barkey heard correctly?

"*No guns,*" the officer repeated.

Eyes wide, Barkey thought: was the man sitting across the table from him serious? Staring sternly at Barkey, the contracting officer had solemnly stated his fifth and final criteria. This caught Barkey completely off balance because he had originally intended to design his new plane not only with the usual missile ordnance but also with a 20mm cannon. With this last revelation, the meeting came to an abrupt end. It had lasted less than twenty minutes. The two men left the room, leaving a bewildered Barkey to ponder his next step. Puzzled and taken aback by this informal and somewhat brusque treatment, Barkey had no option but to acquiesce to the situation. The client is always right, or so the saying goes.

McDonnell Aircraft Company had a strong history of innovative design and a vibrant institutional memory. Producing the first jet aircraft to land on board an aircraft carrier in the late 1940s, McDonnell—which years later acquired Douglas Aircraft Company and which many years later was acquired by Boeing—would exploit this feat and develop a long list of jet fighter aircraft for the U.S. military. Beginning with the FH-1, McDonnell's first production jet fighter, the tradition that was to follow would last into the twenty-first century, with continued development and production of the F-18 Super Hornet now manufactured under the Boeing name.

Faced now with new design parameters, casting any misgivings aside, Barkey accepted the stated criteria and said he understood. Nothing complicated, Barkey thought, but, since he and David Lewis were the primary designers, he knew they had to alter their initial design concept and work out details to accommodate what the Navy now required. Barkey would rely on

his professional expertise and call on McDonnell's experience with the designs of its previous jet aircraft, most notably the swept-wing F-3H Demon.

With the words of the contracting officer, who revealed the Navy's new
fundamental operational demands for the embryonic aircraft, and aware of
size and weight limitations, Barkey and Lewis traded ideas and design con-
cepts. The developmental process progressed.

Lewis, the aerodynamicist, insisted that Barkey keep the air intakes short
and try at all costs to eliminate the tail exhaust housing to reduce weight.
Aerodynamic testing showed that for enhanced roll stability, the tips of the
main wings could be tilted up at about twelve degrees. The rear wings,
called stabilators, were angled down at about twenty-three degrees, creating
what came to be called an "effective wing," and allowed for longitudinal stability at high speeds. Two large square-looking panels, called ramps, were
attached to the fuselage in front of the air intakes on each side. The purpose
of these large plates was two-fold: the fixed intake ramp split the boundary
layer air that lingers along the fuselage during flight from faster moving air,
allowing the fast moving or "clean" air into the intake. Behind the fixed
plate, a variable or rear intake ramp pivoted in and out to restrict the shock
wave generated at supersonic speeds from entering the throat of the intake
and threaten operation of the engines. The vertical tail on the F-4 was long
but short to accommodate the lack of clearance height in the hanger deck.
About amidships of the aircraft, the fuselage was pressed in on both sides to
exploit what came to be known as the "Area Rule." The Area Rule, a critical
aerodynamic concept at high speeds, dictated that as the cross sectional area
of the plane increased, especially through the wing section, the cross section
of the fuselage at that location had to be reduced to compensate for the
added cross-sectional area of the main wing.

Discarding the original plan of using engines with less thrust, Herman
Barkey eventually chose to power the F-4 with two General Electric J-79 engines. The J-79, developed by Gerhard Neumann, was the same engine that
powered the F-104 Starfighter, the B-58 Hustler, and the RA-5C Vigilante.
The hugely powerful J-79 engine, was technically advanced. Weighing about
3,500 pounds, the J-79 consisted of seventeen compressor stages and three
turbine stages. It utilized a single shaft about which turned both the compressor and turbine blades, as well as a radical design that allowed for variable stator (non-rotating) vanes that swiveled and directed airflow. The stator vanes
actually enhanced the plane's acceleration. At seventeen feet in length, the

J-79 was a long, complex power plant system. Positioned side by side in the F-4 and separated by inches, each engine, measuring three feet in diameter, produced about 17,000 pounds of thrust when in afterburner.

Being the key structural engineer, Barkey measured the width of two General Electric J-79 engines that had been placed side by side, and told his design people to give him two inches of wall thickness from the inside of the fuselage to the outside extremity to keep the overall fuselage cross-section as narrow as possible. This was all he would need for structural integrity. Slowly the aircraft began to assume its peculiar, recognizable shape.

Because McDonnell Aircraft Company was awarded the contract from the U.S. Navy, the F-4 began its contractual life, as intended, as a carrier-based plane designed specifically for fleet air defense. It came to evolve that the plane's design would be largely wrapped around the Sparrow missile armament system.

The Sparrow air-to-air missile had a history all its own. The missile was first designed by Sperry Gyroscope Laboratory and Douglas Aircraft Company. Subsequently the Sparrow III emerged and was further designed and manufactured by Raytheon Manufacturing Company. It was the Sparrow III that would become integral to the design and armament of the F-4.

Through the Navy's stated parameters—and the Sparrow missile system and a large radar that necessitated a bulbous nose—the resulting design rendered the F-4 an ungainly, hulking mammoth. Although the aircraft's physical features were indeed strange, the plane was state-of-the-art and would remain so through its many configurations and variations.

The technologically advanced aircraft had begun its laborious path from concept to roll-out, transitioning through numerous changes and variations, including seventy-five wing designs that eventually resulted in a saw-toothed main wing that advanced the outer portion of the wing forward beyond the vortices that are created along the leading edge of the wing. Other considerations included ejection seat selection; modifications in armament and pylons and location of external stores for various ordnance; arresting-hook design; and development of boundary layer control systems.

The plane would assume many cryptic alphanumeric designations and would evolve through many more eventual variants. The military modified the aircraft's alphanumeric designation. Moving forward from the concept of the F-3H, the aircraft began to take shape as the F-3H-C, F-3H-E, and F-3H-G, each originally with a single-seat configuration.

Once the Navy accepted the prototype of the F-3H-G, they changed its designation to AH-1, because they originally saw the plane more as an "attack" aircraft, hence the AH in the alphanumeric designation. But eventually, at the time of the letter of intent, the Navy, considering its new objectives, had developed other ideas. The attack concept gave way to an interceptor for fleet air defense and was redesignated the F-4H-1. But the plane still had no name.

In 1959, late in the aircraft's development years and on the cusp of production, McDonnell Aircraft Company celebrated its twentieth anniversary as a premier American aircraft manufacturing company. From the straight-wing FH-1 Phantom and the F2H Banshee, and through to the design and flight characteristics of the swept-winged F-3H Demon, in which the F-4's new design was partially rooted, Herman Barkey's new plane, now with two seats, neared its final alphanumeric designation. But more importantly, it was to be christened with a new name. The choice of name became obvious. In recognition and honor of McDonnell's first Navy jet-engine fighter, the FH-1 Phantom aircraft, the F-4H-1 was christened the Phantom II.

McDonnell developed two planes under the Phantom II label, which were designated as XF-4H-1 (experimental) and YF-4H-1 (pre-production) aircraft. The aircraft finally emerged simply as the F-4 Phantom II. From that point on, the terms Phantom and F-4 were synonymous and interchangeable.

Many variations of the F-4 were designed with each one being denoted by a different letter after the number "4." F-4Bs were slated for the U.S. Navy and F-4Cs, originally designated as the F-110A, for the U.S. Air Force. Other eventual variants included the F-4D, F-4G, F-4J, F-4M, F-4N, F-4S, RF-4C, RF-4B, and RF-4E. The F-4 was well suited to experimentation, and eventually a variable swept-wing version, the F-4FVS, was conceived but it was never developed beyond the concept stage.

The Navy F-4 was manned by two occupants, the pilot and, behind him, one other person called a Radar Intercept Officer (RIO). In casual parlance, the RIO is often referred to as a "backseater." The RIO manages the radar and navigational functions of the aircraft and is an integral and essential component to the operations of the plane and air defense of the fleet.

Piloted by Robert C. Little, the F-4 Phantom II made its maiden voyage in May of 1958. By the end of the year, McDonnell's plane was considered the Navy's premier all-weather fighter aircraft and entered full development and production.

Throughout its final production variants, the Phantom maintained its profile and to the untrained eye, the differences between variations were difficult to distinguish. The basic physical features would change little from model to model. Each version was mostly the result of interior and systems modifications, most notably radars that required changes in the nose of the aircraft. At some point, at about the "J" version, the aircraft was designed with thicker wings to accommodate fatter tires, but again this was not readily recognizable to the casual observer. Throughout and regardless of its many evolutions, the F-4 remained one of the most easily recognized aircraft.

When the F-4 began to take its final shape and first appeared on the scene, no one knew what to make of it. Awkward in its physical appearance, the F-4 was the subject of many derisive remarks and of a seeming mocking song. The F-4, with its drooped nose, bent saw-toothed wing, and "kicked-in-the-butt" profile, was to some traditionalists a sorry excuse for a jet fighter. These sentiments would quickly change, however, and once production began to accelerate, the F-4 became, in some circles, the benchmark of jet fighter aviation.

Once past testing and in the initial stages of production, first exclusively for the U.S. Navy, the Phantom came to enjoy such a growing reputation that the U.S. Air Force, recognizing its superior speed, flexible capabilities, and maneuverability, was compelled to demand it too. U.S. Secretary of Defense Robert McNamara mandated that the Air Force acquire the aircraft. McDonnell's orders for the aircraft increased overnight with the production rate eventually reaching a peak of ninety-six planes in one month.

The F-4 Phantom II, with two General Electric J-79 engines, set record after record: maximum speed, closed circuit, altitude, sustained altitude, cross-country elapsed times (Los Angeles to New York in less than three hours), time to climb to various altitudes, payload, turning rates, and others. At about fifty-six feet long and about thirty-seven feet wide, wingtip to wingtip, the plane was large, heavy, and seemingly cumbersome.

The bland description of the F-4, as paraphrased from the NATOPS (Naval Air Training and Operating Procedures Standardization) Flight Manual, belies the true essence, mystique, and appeal of the aircraft:

> The F-4 aircraft is a two-place (tandem) supersonic long-range, all-weather fighter built by McDonnell Aircraft Company. The aircraft uses missiles as the principal armament for intermediate or long-range interceptions. The aircraft features a low-mounted, swept-

back wing with anhedral at the wingtips, and a one-piece stabilator with cathedral, mounted low on the aft fuselage. The pressurized cockpit is enclosed by two clamshell canopies.

From the F-4's evolutionary beginnings with the F-3 Demon in 1945, Herman Barkey designed and eventually built what would become the second most prolific jet fighter or fighter/bomber in US history. During the production years of 1959 to 1979, a little over 5,000 F-4s were manufactured and assembled in McDonnell's St. Louis plant, located adjacent to parallel runways at Lambert Field. The F-86 Sabre Jet, with over 9,000 planes manufactured, remains to this day, the most prolific American jet fighter ever manufactured.

With the exception of those made in Japan under license, every F-4 that saw service originated from St. Louis. Placed nose to tail, the total production of F-4s would stretch for more than fifty-three miles.

But for all its advantages, the F-4 also had some drawbacks and deficiencies due to a role it was destined to have but for which it had not been designed to fulfill. No plane can be all things to all people. Aircraft design is really one of compromise. Among its shortcomings, the Phantom could sustain its Mach speed for only a few moments before it ran out of fuel. Second, it left a telltale trail of highly visible smoke from its exhaust. Third, aft vision was restricted. The fourth and perhaps most significant disadvantage was that the original air defense concept as promulgated by the Navy did not include machine guns or 20mm cannons. The Phantom had been developed to attack its adversaries at a distance beyond or at the edge of visual range and relied on the Sparrow and Sidewinder missiles. The design did not anticipate close air combat. The F-4 Phantom II found itself in unfriendly skies over North Vietnam and had no option but to fulfill this role. Only years later, was a 20mm "gatling gun" cannon finally installed in the nose of the Phantom.

Until the variable wing F-111 Aardvark and the B-52 Stratofortress were introduced to the air war in the skies over North Vietnam, the F-4 was the most coveted target and prized shoot-down of every North Vietnamese gunner and missile-man. Because of the telltale plume of dark smoke streaming behind the F-4, the Vietnamese called it *"Vi ruoi"* (pronounced, vee-joy), which is Vietnamese for "fly swatter." From the ground, the smoke trail that appeared attached to the plane resembled the handle of a flyswatter, and the plane the swatter itself. The North Vietnamese also called the F-4 *"Con ma,"* which means ghost or phantom. Every North Vietnamese antiaircraft gunner wanted to shoot down a *Vi ruoi, a Con ma.*

Chapter 7

Deciphering the Indecipherable: U.S. Navy F-4 Phantom II Aircraft Markings during the Vietnam War

THE MARKINGS AND COLOR SCHEMES OF THE U.S. Navy F-4 Phantoms differed from those of the U.S. Air Force. Whereas the U.S. Air Force eventually adopted darker, camouflaged colors with which the Navy briefly experimented, the Navy F-4s, in stark contrast, were painted light gray (or off-white) on top with their underbelly and under-wings painted white.

The star insignia on each side of the fuselage and on the wings of Navy F-4s, evolved from the early 1900s. The evolution was complicated with quite a few variations, some of which were unofficial. The first insignia was round with a white, five-pointed star inset with a red disk inset inside the star. Over the decades the red disk was eliminated and a white, five-pointed star was inset in a blue circle. Later, in 1943, a white rectangle was placed on each side of the blue circle and white star and the entire insignia was encircled with red. Finally, in 1947, the insignia that emerged and would eventually appear on the F-4, consisted of a blue circle with a white, five-pointed star inset and a rectangle placed to either side of the circle with a red horizontal stripe in the middle of each rectangle. A blue line marked the perimeter of the entire insignia.

The Navy employed various numeric and alphanumeric identification markings and marked their F-4s in three ways. First, the last four digits of a six-digit number that constituted the bureau number—the serial number—were painted on each side of the plane just above the exhaust in large black numbers that were readily seen. The bureau number, which remains with the plane for its entire life, never varying, has a long history.

When the bureau numbering system began in about 1940, it contained five digits, but later, as production swelled, the number was expanded to six digits. For Navy and Marine Corps aircraft, the bureau number is assigned to the aircraft at date of order, not date of delivery. Generally speaking, with some exceptions notwithstanding production blocks and cancellations, the bureau number is the most significant identifier of any aircraft in the Navy's inventory. It allows the aircraft to be tracked throughout its service life.

The name of the carrier off which the planes operated was also stenciled on the sides near the crest of the fuselage.

Identifying each plane within a squadron was accomplished with a three-digit serialized number referred to as the side number, or modex. Three-digit numbers beginning in "1" (101, 102, etc.) or "2" (201, 202, etc.), in general, but not always, were reserved for the fighter squadrons and three-digit numbers beginning with "3," "4" or "5" were reserved for planes in other than fighter squadrons. The F-4 side number appeared in front of each air intake and on the top surface of the right wing. Pilots referred to each plane through its three-digit side number, which was, for them, more important than the Bureau Number. In fact, it was their principal identifier for each plane.

The air wing to which all aircraft aboard a carrier belonged was identified by two letters. The two-letter grouping was referred to as the tail code and, after many variations and years of evolution, came into effect around 1957. The second letter identified the specific air wing and the first letter whether the air wing operated from the West Coast or the East Coast. West Coast air wings were designated with an "N," whereas East Coast air wings were denoted with an "A." The letters "NH" in block print, appearing on the vertical stabilizer and on the top surface of the right wing next to the side number, told the observer that Air wing Eleven (H) operated from the West Coast (N). In the case of NH, the air wing's aircraft flew from the USS *Kitty Hawk*.

Not visible, but heard and referred to often, was a code name or, more accurately, a call sign for the squadron. For example, although VF-114 was called the "Aardvarks," their call sign was "Linfield."

Chapter 8
Last Chance for Survival: The Ejection Seat

REALIZING THAT PILOTS NEEDED A MEANS TO escape military air-craft quickly and safely, toward the end of World War II, researchers began experimenting with the development of an ejection seat. With the exception of the overall aircraft itself, the ejection seat is perhaps the most intriguing system of all. A silent, seemingly inert system, unseen by the casual ob-server, the seat may never be activated. Once it is, however, there is no room for trial and error. The ejection seat must operate under a variety of situations. It must take into account many variables, the most important be-ing the physiology and physical limitations of the human being. It must act and react in concert with the survival needs of the pilot and in a manner that is reliable. When the system is activated, there must be no equivoca-tion, no hesitation; it must perform as intended and without fail. The fate of the airman is dependent on it.

The F-4 Phantom IIs were equipped with the Mark 5 ejection seat system developed and designed by the Martin-Baker Aircraft Company, located west of London near Uxbridge, England.

Without delving into the history of the ejection seat, which is in itself col-orful, it is safe to say that by the time the F-4 Phantom II arrived on the scene in St. Louis, ejection seat design was pretty far along. It was an ad-vanced piece of equipment integral with the plane itself; but even then, new strides in improvement were already underway.

Martin-Baker maintains records of ejections that involve their ejection seats. The company lists, on a bulletin board in their corporate reception lobby, the most recent ejections with photos of the types of planes, if not photos of the very planes themselves. Martin-Baker considers a seat ejection to be successful if airmen survive the ejection, the landing, and any injuries they may have sustained during the ejection. Martin-Baker always strives for the highest of quality control and total reliability of its ejection seat systems. They know that airmen must feel confident that they can rely on their product one hundred percent—that they can escape from an emergency situation, and that their chances of survival come with a very high probability of success.

To activate, or fire, the Mark 5 ejection seat, all one has to do is reach up and pull a firing handle—a stiff, looped cord—down over one's head, which also pulls a thick canvas face curtain over the pilot's facemask. If a pilot is disabled or unable to reach the overhead handle, as an alternative, the pilot could pull up on a second handle (again, a looped D-ring) that is situated between the pilot's knees. These handles are easily identifiable, easily accessible. There is no time to waste during an emergency.

Then once the handle is pulled, it sets off a series of actions that are interlinked, interdependent and irreversible. The pilot now is at the mercy of the ejection process itself.

Seen in film footage of various seat ejections, the ejection process occurs very quickly—the pilot is in the cockpit one second and floating aloft beneath an open parachute the next. But the short ejection duration does not readily reveal the sequential, intricate process or what transpires to render the pilot safely out of his cockpit.

Because of the dynamics involved—the plane's attitude, atmospheric conditions, altitude, speed, even the airman's weight—the design of the ejection seat must account for many factors. For instance, should a pilot eject at high altitude (say 50,000 feet) and his parachute opens, he would not survive due to extremely frigid temperatures (and lack of oxygen). The slow rate of descent would cause him to freeze to death. The seat is designed to compensate for this by delaying activation of the parachute until the pilot has descended to a more hospitable altitude.

One of the most famous photographs of the Vietnam War, taken 24 April 1967, captured James (Jimmy) Laing just ejecting from the back seat of an F-4 piloted by Charles Everett Southwick. The photo was taken by Gary Anderson, an RIO of another F-4, piloted by Hugh Dennis (Denny) Wisely of the same squadron (VF-114). The photograph clearly shows Laing out of the cockpit still in his seat tilted forward, with what looks like a rail probe extending vertically up from his F-4 below him and behind the cockpit where his seat had once been. The rail-like extension is really a tube. The tube extension is in fact a sort of gun barrel that serves as the catapult to propel the seat carrying the pilot upward and safely out of the aircraft.

In 1967, the Mark 5 employed, as the propellant, three sequential explosive charges placed in the tube with each charge being separated by a diaphragm. The expanding gases from these charges would launch the ejection seat. The reason for the three charges is that the human body is too frail to withstand the acceleration loads required to overcome the inertia of a stationary body and accelerate it to the desired velocity and safely clear the aircraft tail. Realizing the size of charge needed to propel a man out of a plane, Martin-Baker quickly learned that the spine or backbone of the human being cannot comfortably withstand the sudden impulse of high acceleration. So the explosions inside a telescoping gun tube were divided into three zones. As the explosion in the initial zone within the telescoping gun occurred, the hot gases would expand, extending the pistons and unlocking the seat. The hot gas of the initial explosion burns through the diaphragm and ignites the second explosive charge, extending a second piston concentric with the first, and so on until all three charges are detonated in rapid succession. The use of progressive charges produces a more constant acceleration that the human spine can withstand. But the process occurs so fast that it would all sound like one explosion.

Today, most ejection seats are of the rocket type, the thrust of which augments and dispenses with the catapult barrel seen in the Laing photograph. The primary advantage of the rocket-propelled system is that it provides for a smooth transition from catapult to rocket propulsion, thereby reducing the sudden impulse to the airman's body.

As soon as the airman pulls the ejection handle of a Mark 5 ejection seat, either from over his head or from between his knees, the canopy is blown off and immediately two things happen: a leg restraint system—which an airman would already have attached prior to flight—consisting of garters around the calves and a line that connects the garters back to the seat, restrains his legs from flailing during ejection. Also, his seat shoulder harness locks his torso tightly. Secondly, fractions of a second later, the three charges go off in the telescopic tube and the hot gases from the explosions extend the tube propelling the ejection seat and the airman out of the top of the aircraft. About half a second after the seat is ejected, another smaller explosion occurs at the left rear of the seat, which propels a heavy projectile out. This projectile pulls out a drogue chute, located immediately behind the pilot's head, that stabilizes the ejection seat. After one-and-a-half seconds, or when speed and altitude dictate (as controlled by a barostatic time release unit, or BTRU), the drogue chute pulls out the main chute, and the main chute opens. As a last sequence of the process, the straps and harnesses securing the airman to his seat are automatically released and the airman is pulled out of and freed from the ejection seat. The airman descends safely beneath his parachute, complete with a survival kit. The entire process takes less than three seconds.

Chapter 9
Flameout or Compressor Stall

JET ENGINES, FOR ALL THEIR RELIABILITY, are vulnerable. They function well only if design parameters are observed, particularly those that address air supply and airflow. A large part of designing a jet engine is the understanding of the flight characteristics of an aircraft, its flight environment and operating limitations, and the parameters, or performance envelope, in which the engine must operate. Altitude, angle of attack of the plane, angle of attack of each compressor and turbine blade, and whether operating in level flight or at takeoff or landing, or at slow or fast speeds, the engine must operate in the manner intended for a given set of circumstances. Exceeding the design parameters or operating outside the performance envelope is critical and will result in something other than efficient operation of the engine; or in catastrophe itself.

Inherent in the design of fighter jets, special provisions are made for sophisticated, high-performance jet engines. Unlike commercial jet liners where the engines are slung beneath the wings, the engines for a jet fighter are enclosed within the fuselage. There are several reasons for this but one is the need for variable geometry of the air intake. Although not part of the engine itself, the air intake of a jet fighter, which is integral with the fuselage, is an essential part of the entire airflow system. Modern jet fighters can fly at supersonic speeds but the engines that propel them cannot ingest air and then burn the air and fuel mixture at these speeds. Ingestion of the sonic wave is detrimental to a jet engine. Hence the air intake of a jet fighter must compensate for supersonic, transonic, and subsonic airflow.

At some point prior to the compressor face of the engine, supersonic airflow must be slowed to subsonic speeds before it enters the engine. Without knowing its modern-day application, Daniel Bernoulli (1700-1782) and Antoine Lavoisier (1743-1794) and, before them, Rene Descartes (1596-1650) understood the principle centuries ago. Based on the law of conservation of energy and the law of continuity, their equations provided for the key aspect of intake design: for a continuous, uninterrupted system, in general, the volumetric flow of air (or liquid for that matter) at any point in the system must be the same at any other point. Application of Bernoulli's theory follows a simple principle. To slow supersonic air to subsonic speeds, at some point just in front of the engine, in an area referred to as the bell house, the cross-sectional area is enlarged. The same volumetric flow of air is maintained but the velocity of the air is reduced.

Other than a mechanical or electrical malfunction, jet engines are susceptible to a phenomenon known as "compressor stall." A jet engine is divided into several independent yet interdependent compartments: compressor section, combustion chamber, turbine section, and exhaust. In an overly simplified representation, the compressor section is a series of plates that are serrated at the edge like a fan. The serrations are, in fact, the blades that move the air aft. Each stage of the compressor moves air faster longitudinally, thereby compressing it and, abiding by the laws of thermodynamics, heating it. The blades at each stage become smaller; the resulting compression becomes higher. The high velocity air is then forced into a combustion chamber (can) where it is mixed with atomized fuel. The fuel-air mixture ignites in a continuous controlled flame. The expanding gases are forced backward into the turbine section where the gases continue to expand and spin the turbine, which is the driving force behind the compressor. The result is thrust. Thrust equals force and for every force, as Isaac Newton (1642-1727) observed and which became known as his third law of motion, there is a counter force. The counter force, in this case, since nothing is pushing against the thrust, is the forward movement of the plane. Other forces, of course, such as gravity, lift, drag, and inertia of the mass itself have an effect on the plane too.

Compressor and turbine blades are small airfoils, which act like the wings of a plane, but not quite. In stable, sustained flight, a wing may stall if the angle of attack is such that the wing no longer provides lift. In such a case, streamlines of airflow over the top of the wing have become detached from the wing and the pressure differential between top and bottom, which gives lift, equalizes. In other words, the pressure above the wing is now the same as the pressure beneath the wing. The airfoil stalls. The same dynamic is at work with the blades of a compressor. But, whereas airfoils or wings process rectilinear air, compressor blades process air in two ways. First there is the rectilinear or axial airflow but secondly, as the blades chew into the air, there is a rotational airflow. So not only are the blades convex (or concave, depending on one's reference), they are also twisted at a slight angle.

Compressor stall occurs when the flow of air through the compressor section of the engine is such that the streamlines of the airflow separate from the back, or convex, side of the compressor blade, thereby creating a small cell of stale air immediately behind each blade. Multiplied by many hundreds of blades spinning very fast, collectively these stagnant cells are enough to disrupt the combustion farther back in the engine.

Given the relatively small size of the compressor blades in a jet engine and the high speed at which they rotate, compressor stall is difficult to imagine. Nature slows down the process and provides a simplified analogy of compressor stall: the same principle is at work with the bend in a river. On the upstream side of the river bend, the faster flow of water is uninterrupted and tends to gouge out the bank. On the downstream, or lee side, of the bend, the faster flow separates from the bend, in essence is no longer "attached," and tends away from the bend, allowing for stiller water near the bend itself. This is why sand deposits are often seen downstream of a bend in a river.

But there is one distinctive characteristic associated with compressor stall: a loud unmistakable *bang* in the engine. This bang is sometimes accompanied by a large flame rushing out not only from the rear of the engine but out the front too. At thousands of revolutions per minute, a jet engine's compressor blades, if at stall, will immediately fail to produce airflow sufficient for controlled combustion in the combustion chamber. Without benefit of controlled airflow, the fuel-air mixture being ignited in the combustion chamber is now free to explode in all directions, and flames shoot out the front of the intake of the jet engine, resulting in flameout.

Flameout is an unfortunate choice of words. In its most elemental definition, flameout means the flame in the engine has been extinguished. Shutting down the engine or a lack of fuel or the denial of oxygen will automatically extinguish the flame. Also, early jet engine designers realized that the faster a plane flies, the farther back the combustion flame is pushed. Conceptually, if the flame leaves the rear of the engine, it is no longer contained in the combustion chamber and flames out. But these scenarios are technically not flameouts as they relate to compressor stall.

Chapter 10
Knows neither Friend nor Foe: The Zuni Rocket

WITH THE EXCEPTION OF NUCLEAR, nerve gas, and biological weapons (Agent Orange notwithstanding), the United States made use of its entire weapons inventory while engaged in Vietnam. Ordnance ranged from small-caliber pistol rounds to large sixteen-inch-diameter shells from the battleship USS *New Jersey* (BB-62); from baseball-sized, handheld grenades to 2,000-pound bombs and giant, large-diameter bombs called "daisy cutters." Daisy cutters, dropped from the back of C-130 cargo planes, were intended to clear an area of dense jungle two hundred feet in diameter immediately to create a helicopter landing zone.

While planes dropped bombs and napalm and helicopters sprayed an area with machine-gun fire and small rockets, the cluster bomb unit (CBU) and the Zuni rocket, depending on the target, were highly effective, anti-personnel, air-to-ground weapons.

The Zuni rocket filled the void between bullets and bombs and caused devastation on a sizable scale. American ground troops favorably regarded the Zuni rocket because of the immediate saturation and destructive coverage of a large geographic area as a result of multiple detonations of several Zunis fired at the same time.

Containing an internal explosive charge powerful enough to destroy a building, the Zuni rocket was intended to decimate or annihilate ground forces and to render equipment unusable by exploding above or on impact with the ground. The resulting spread of hot shrapnel over a large area cut down personnel within its range of effectiveness.

The Zuni rocket is five inches in diameter and about eight feet long. It is launched from cylindrical pods. Each pod carries four Zuni rockets each contained in its own tube. The rocket pods (or packs) are carried beneath the wings of an aircraft, sometimes from triple ejector racks (TERs) with three pods per rack. The F-4B, practically speaking, could carry ten pods, five beneath each wing, for a total of forty rockets.

Prior to flight, each rocket is slid into its tube with its fins folded. Once fired, the fins spring out and provide stability for the rocket's trajectory. The rockets are unguided and fly a predetermined path as established by the pilot's control of the plane.

Once armed by the arming switch in the cockpit on an F-4, Zuni rockets are fired simply by depressing a button on the control stick. Zuni rockets are fired in small incremental divisions of time or, if the time increments are reduced, in what could be considered a salvo. Once fired, the lightweight launch tube or pod is empty and can be jettisoned from the plane or reused.

Quickly reaching a speed of about 900 miles per hour (Mach 1.4), Zuni rockets, if seen from the ground, race away from the front of the plane faster than the human eye can register the movement. They leave behind thick exhaust from their solid propellant rocket motors that burn out within seconds.

Although air-to-ground (close air support or flak suppression) eventually became the primary role for the Zuni rocket, it was originally considered an air-to-air rocket as well.

Zuni rockets fired from an F-8 were evidently a contributing factor in the downing of a MiG-17 in July of 1967. For those who may be skeptical, the other contributing factor may have been the plane's 20mm cannon. Nonetheless, the pilot did shoot down a MiG, a fact that, regardless of weapon, cannot be denied.

About three months earlier, Theodore Swartz, firing three Zuni rockets while flying an A-4C Skyhawk with VA-76, unmistakably and undeniably shot down a MiG-17. There is also a report of an Israeli pilot having accomplished the same feat in the Middle East.

True of all ordnance, the Zuni rocket can distinguish neither friend nor foe and once launched, there will be consequences. Sometimes the benefits do not accrue as intended and the results can be ruinous.

Since the 1960s, four major mishaps involving missiles and rockets have occurred aboard U.S. aircraft carriers. One incident, which killed more than forty sailors, resulted from the detonation of a 2.75-inch rocket placed in a locker on the USS *Oriskany* (CVA-34). The other involved the detonation of a Sparrow missile lodged in burning debris aboard the USS *Nimitz* (CVN-68) in the aftermath of the crash of an E-6B, which resulted in the death of fourteen sailors.

The other two incidences involved Zuni rockets. Twenty-eight sailors lost their lives in January 1969 on the USS *Enterprise* when an explosion of a Zuni rocket occurred. The exhaust from an aircraft starter unit heated the rocket's warhead and caused it to detonate. Three more Zuni warheads eventually exploded, causing havoc.

In each of these three carrier/missile/rocket mishaps, the missiles or rockets were stationary. It was the fourth incident, however, on board the USS *Forrestal* in late July 1967, that the worst of the four tragedies unfolded. Incredibly, a Zuni rocket carried by an F-4 was accidentally launched, perhaps by a stray electrical current. Passing through the body of a deck crewman, it slammed into a fully fueled and fully armed A-4 Skyhawk. The Skyhawk's pilot was LCDR John McCain, who became a Republican senator from Arizona and, forty-one years later, a presidential candidate. More than one hundred thirty sailors died and another one hundred sixty were injured that day in the resulting carnage of what was probably the worst fire on board a carrier in history. The USS *Forrestal* never saw action again in the waters off Vietnam.

Chapter 11
Ev Southwick, Pilot; Jack Rollins, Radar Intercept Officer

BY 1967, THEN LTCDR CHARLES EVERETT "EV" SOUTHWICK and LT David John "Jack" Rollins had enjoyed distinguished careers in the U.S. Navy.

Ev Southwick received his commission in the U.S. Navy and his naval aviator wings on 14 April 1955. A native of Fairbanks, Alaska, born in 1931, Ev attended high school in Seattle and eventually graduated with a Bachelor of Arts degree with a major in history from the University of Washington. Continuing with his high school athletic training, Ev became a star athlete at the University of Washington, lettering in track and field. He was a sprinter and ran the quarter mile (what was then called the "four-forty").

During summer months while attending the university, he worked in Southeast Alaska at a remote salmon cannery on Prince of Wales Island in several capacities, including that of storekeeper at the company store. Ex–World War II navy pilots had formed an airline company that serviced the island and surrounding area. Ev would meet their amphibious Grumman Goose aircraft arriving at the island to assist passengers and to load and offload supplies and mail. He became friends with the pilots. On several occasions they took him with them on short round trips to other destinations. Seated in the co-pilot's seat, Ev was allowed to operate the controls.

Ev had always shown an interest in aviation. When he was young he built model airplanes. Now, with this real experience, Ev became keenly interested in flying. Back at the University of Washington, some of his fraternity brothers from Alpha Delta Phi went into the U.S. Navy flight training program at Pensacola, Florida. One day about this time, Ev and his cousin were sitting on a rooftop in Seattle and watched as F-9F Panther jets of the Navy Blue Angels flew overhead. Ev said to himself, *I want to do that*. He followed the example of his fraternity brothers and was accepted into the navy flight training program at Pensacola.

Ev flew the FJ-3 Fury and the F-8 Crusader before transitioning to the F-4B Phantom II in October of 1966. He joined VF-114 as a replacement operations officer during *Kitty Hawk*'s 1966-67 cruise to the Tonkin Gulf. Prior to his cruise on the USS *Kitty Hawk*, Ev made cruises on the USS *Bon Homme Richard*, the USS *Midway*, the USS *Constellation*, and the USS *Ticonderoga*.

David John "Jack" Rollins was born in Oakland, California in May 1931. After graduating from high school in 1948, he enlisted in the U.S. Navy, where he served as an enlisted aircrewman and advanced to the rank of Chief Petty Officer. Jack was commissioned as a limited duty officer in 1960 and was assigned to the F-4 Phantom II Fleet Introduction Team as a Radar Intercept Officer. He was then assigned to VF-114, the first F-4 Phantom II squadron. After completing his tour, he was assigned to VF-121 as a flight instructor. Except for two short tours, one on the East Coast and one in Texas, Jack was assigned to squadrons at the Naval Air Station, north of San Diego, California—NAS Miramar. He made cruises on the USS *Valley Forge* (CVA-45), the USS *Ticonderoga*, the USS *Shangri-La* (CVS-38), the USS *Oriskany* and the USS *Kitty Hawk*. He then rejoined VF-114 in August of 1966, and embarked on a second cruise aboard *Kitty Hawk* later that year as a RIO for his second tour to Vietnam.

Câu Hàm Rồng trước ngày tiêu thổ kháng chiến

The first Ham Rong Bridge, considered the most beautiful structure to adorn French Indo-China, was designed and built by the French. The bridge was destroyed by the Viet Minh in 1945. Note the hillock "Nui Ngoc" (Jade Mountain) in the background

Nguyen Dinh Doan (*right*) explains the intricacies of bridge design and construction to Pham Van Dong, Premier of North Vietnam (*center*) at the dedication of the second (re-built) Ham Rong bridge in 1964. (Photo courtesy Nguyen Dinh Doan)

Nguyen Dinh Doan (*far left*) at the dedication ceremony of the second Ham Rong (Thanh Hoa) Bridge on 19 May 1964, Ho Chi Minh's birthday. This structure replaced the steel double-arch, single-span bridge destroyed in 1945. (Photo courtesy Nguyen Dinh Doan)

The stamp designed by Do Viet Tuan, published by Tien Bo Printing House, to commemorate the dedication on 19 May 1964 of the second Ham Rong (Thanh Hoa) Bridge designed and built by Nguyen Dinh Doan. Translation reads: "People's Republic of Vietnam"

Benchmark and precise location marker of the entrance to the
Ham Rong Bridge (170 kilometers and 478 meters south of Hanoi)

Nguyen Dinh Doan, civil engineer and designer of the
second and third Ham Rong Bridges, at his home in
Hanoi, 2002. He's holding a picture of the bridge en-
graved in granite

Ham Rong Bridge, 1967. This photo was developed from the negative reversed. (U.S. Navy photo, courtesy Naval History and Heritage Command)

Ham Rong Bridge, date unknown, but believed to be circa 1967. (U.S. Navy photo, courtesy Naval History and Heritage Command)

A 37mm antiaircraft gun. During the war, the North Vietnamese made use of more than 10,000 of these guns, which
proved to be most effective against American planes

A ZPU-44 (14.5mm) multi-barrel antiaircraft machine gun.
These were very effective and very mobile, with a high rate
of fire

A 57mm North Vietnamese antiaircraft gun, believed to be near Thanh Hoa, circa 1967. (Photo courtesy Istvan Toperczer, Hungary)

A North Vietnamese 37mm antiaircraft gun crew near Thanh Hoa, believed to be circa 1967

A North Vietnamese antiaircraft gunner feeds 37mm shells into the breach of an antiaircraft gun from the top. The 37mm gun fires five shots at a time from a clip and was prolific around the Thanh Hoa Bridge in 1967

Although the North Vietnamese surrounded the Ham Rong Bridge with land based antiaircraft artillery, they also defended it using boat-mounted antiaircraft weaponry

A Russian-made surface to air missile (SAM) at the Air Defense/Air Force Museum in Hanoi

HÌNH DẠNG
MỘT SỐ MÁY BAY ĐỊCH

Hình1_ MÁY BAY TIÊM KÍCH F 4 H-1 (F.4 B)

71

The North Vietnamese tried to educate the citizenry of North Vietnam about American airplanes. Here is a sketch from a publicly distributed aircraft identification manual that depicts an F-4B Phantom II, circa 1966-67

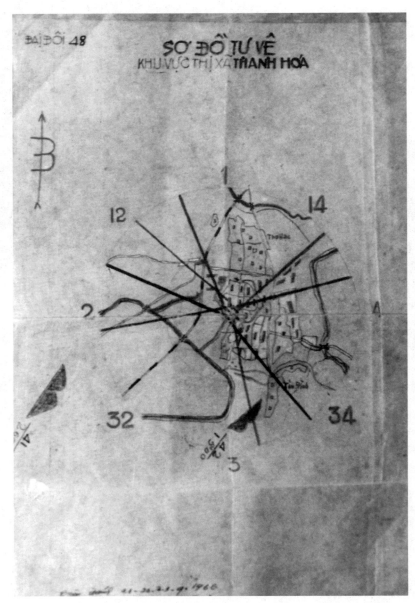

A 1966 North Vietnamese map drawn on parchment with colored pencils showing the defense of and evacuation plan for Thanh Hoa during the Vietnam War

The USS *Kitty Hawk* (at that time, CVA-63) in the Gulf of Tonkin during her 1966-67 Westpac cruise. Positioned on the flight deck are A-3s, A-4s, an RA-5C and, on the port side near the bow, F-4 Phantoms from VF-114 and VF-213. A-6s are not visible. (U.S. Navy photo, courtesy Denny Wisely)

Overhead view of an F-4 Phantom II of VF-101. F-4 Phantom IIs first arrived in Southeast Asia aboard the USS *Constellation* and USS *Midway* about mid-1964 and at Ubon Air Base in Thailand in mid-1965. The first loss of an F-4 in Southeast Asia occurred in mid-November 1964 (Navy). That was followed a few months later by one in early April (Navy) and another in June (Air Force) 1965. But these losses were operational in nature. The first combat loss of an F-4 Phantom II over North Vietnam occurred on 20 June 1965, flown by then U.S. Air Force Capt. Paul A. Kari with Capt. Curt H. Briggs in the backseat as WSO. The plane, belonging to the 45th Tactical Fighter Squadron of the 15th Tactical Fighter Wing from Ubon, Thailand, was hit by antiaircraft fire while on a bombing mission near Son La west of Hanoi. Ironically, the brand new F-4 had just been ferried from the U.S. and had less than twenty-five hours flying time. Two months later, in August 1965, on a mission near the Thanh Hoa Bridge, the U.S. Navy lost its first F-4 Phantom II as a result of combat. Piloted by CDR Frederick A. Franke, with LCDR Robert H. Doremus as Franke's RIO from VF-21 (Freelancers) off the USS *Midway*, the Navy F-4 was downed by a SAM missile. While Capt. Briggs evaded capture and was rescued, Capt. Kari, CDR Franke and LCDR Doremus became prisoners of war. They would be released from North Vietnam in early spring 1973. Approximately six hundred seventy F-4 Phantom IIs, from the combined services, were lost during the conflict in all of Southeast Asia. (U.S. Navy photo, by M. Hershenson, courtesy Naval History and Heritage Command)

An F-4 Phantom II landing aboard the USS *Forrestal* (CVA-59) in February 1967. (U.S. Navy photo, courtesy Naval History and Heritage Command)

An F-4 Phantom II under assembly at the McDonnell Aircraft Company manufacturing facility in St. Louis, circa late 1960s, where five thousand F-4 Phantoms were manufactured. McDonnell purchased Douglas Aircraft Company and was later acquired by Boeing. (U.S. Navy photo, courtesy Naval History and Heritage Command)

Herman D. Barkey, principal designer of the F-4 Phantom II, in his study at his home in Chesterfield, Missouri in late summer 2002. Mr. Barkey, born in 1909, passed away in December 2005. He is survived by his daughter Bonnie Barkey Moore. Firmly molded by the engineering discipline, rooted in strict engineering design criteria and an expert with a slide rule—what was then, before the computer age, the symbol of engineering—Mr. Barkey was an "engineer's engineer." He led the design of the F-4 from concept to roll-out and through many of its variations. So committed was he to the Phantom, that it consumed his life. During the author's interview with Mr. Barkey, a retiring individual not given to boasting or self-adulation, at first he was reluctant to discuss the plane, But as he became comfortable with the conversation, a broad grin crossing his face, pride showing brightly in his eyes, Mr. Barkey became lively and forthcoming with discussion about and descriptions of his passion, the F-4 Phantom II. Sometimes brusque with his design team, sometimes aloof, a no-nonsense professional, he displayed moments of deep compassion for those who worked for him. Recognizing that a plane as sophisticated as the F-4 cannot be designed alone, he knew he needed the loyalty of his designers and took care of them. In a pensive moment during the interview, a side of Herman Barkey, not often seen, revealed itself. *"I knew we were designing the best fighter jet the world had ever seen but I knew it was still vulnerable; all planes are."* In deeper thought: *"When we began the design of the F-4, we had no idea there would be a war in Vietnam or that the Phantom would play such an important role in it."* Now reflective, somewhat sullen, his clear eyes fixed on some distant, imaginary point, he paused and then continued: *"We lost a lot of them over there, didn't we?"*

Front cockpit of an F-4 Phantom II, similar to what Ev Southwick would have observed. *Middle, from top down*: the radar scope, ADI and HSI are clearly visible. Note the twin vertical rows of engine instruments at the right

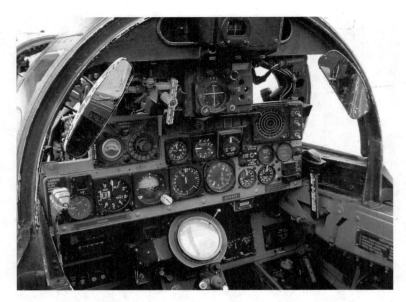

Back cockpit of an F-4 Phantom II. Although not exactly the same, this is similar to the visual environment Jack Rollins would have experienced in the backseat of Linfield Two Zero One

Pilots and Radar Intercept Officers of VF-114 on the 1966-67 cruise to the Gulf of Tonkin. Jack Rollins is 5th from the left in the back row. Ev South-wick was not present for the photograph; he joined the squadron later in the cruise. (U.S. Navy photo, courtesy Denny Wisely)

An F-4 Phantom II is positioned, as a display, on the starboard bow catapult on the USS *Yorktown* (CVA-10) in Charleston, South Carolina

Zuni rocket pod with four Zuni rockets beneath the wing of an A-4 Skyhawk on the flight deck of the USS *Midway* Museum in San Diego, California

A Zuni rocket on display at the Smithsonian Institution Air and Space Museum in Chantilly, Virginia

An F-4 Phantom II from VF-143 (Pukin' Dogs) fires Zuni Rockets at a target off the coast of Vietnam in 1966. (U.S. Navy photo, courtesy Naval History and Heritage Command)

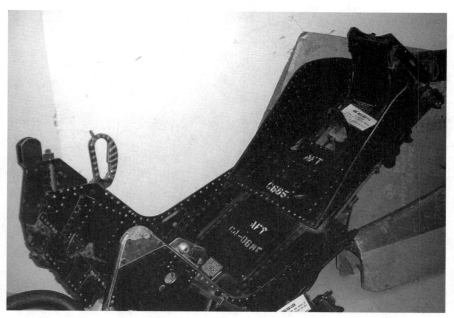

The frame of a Martin-Baker Mark 5 ejection seat from an F-4 Phantom II, photographed in Hanoi

Ev Southwick preparing to enter his F-8 Crusader. Ev flew the FJ-3 Fury and the F-8 Crusader before transitioning to the F-4B Phantom II in October of 1966. Ev joined VF-114 as a replacement operations officer during the *Kitty Hawk's* '66-'67 cruise to the Tonkin Gulf. Ev made cruises on the *Bon Homme Richard, Midway, Constellation* and *Ticonderoga.* (Photo courtesy Ev Southwick and Jack Rollins)

Chapter 12
Fate Is the Hunter

BEGINNING IN NOVEMBER 1966, THE SECOND combat deployment to the Gulf of Tonkin for the USS *Kitty Hawk* and Air Wing Eleven, under the respective commands of CAPT Paul Pugh and CDR Henry Urban, had not been uneventful. *Kitty Hawk* and Air Wing Eleven, since their arrival in the Gulf of Tonkin, had endured relentless, arduous combat against enemy targets and the air defenses of North Vietnam. Now, in mid-May 1967, some six months into the cruise, with thousands of sorties launched from the deck of *Kitty Hawk* and hundreds of successfully completed missions, to the credit of her air wing, a sense of pride and elation prevailed on the mighty warship.

But while the pride was evident, the elation was tempered. The previous months of combat had also resulted in many disasters. Carrier operations are inherently dangerous; combat operations even more so. The vagaries of war being what they are, combat and operational losses had taken a heavy toll on equipment and aircrews.

Two weeks into her first line period, on 21 December 1966, ten days shy of the new year, *Kitty Hawk* suffered her first loss. An A-4C Skyhawk attack aircraft of VA-144 was shot down by antiaircraft fire while on a reconnaissance mission over Highway 1. The pilot ejected safely but was captured by the North Vietnamese.

After a little less than two months into *Kitty Hawk*'s cruise, 1966 slipped into history, giving way to 1967. Remaining on station and having to observe Christmas and New Year's in the waters off North Vietnam, the crews of *Kitty Hawk* and Air Wing Eleven would celebrate the New Year a few days later in the Philippines, where routine maintenance and replenishment would take place at Subic Bay.

Kitty Hawk's air losses to that point had been minimal. But entering the worst year for American air combat losses in Vietnam, her luck was about to change. Although the old year had ended, *Kitty Hawk*'s losses would not.

By mid-January 1967, *Kitty Hawk* and her air wing had left Subic Bay and returned to combat for their second line period of the cruise in the Gulf of Tonkin off the shores of North Vietnam.

The air wing's second line period and first days of combat in 1967 began with the loss of a two-man crew A-6 Intruder aircraft of VA-85 downed by antiaircraft fire north of Thanh Hoa on the 19th of January. On the same day, an F-4B from VF-114 experienced engine failure during a catapult launch and crashed into the water, killing both crewmen. A day later, on 20 January, an A-4 from VA-112 was hit possibly by small-arms fire over North Vietnam and crashed not far from Thanh Hoa. The pilot was killed. During the first week in February, on the 4th to be exact, an F-4B was lost due to unknown reasons northeast of Thanh Hoa. Its crew was never found.

Kitty Hawk left her second line period in late February and repaired to Subic Bay and Hong Kong, again for replenishment and maintenance. Once the ship returned to Yankee Station for further combat operations, the air wing sustained further losses.

An A-3 Skywarrior of Detachment C of VAH-4 was lost on 8 March 1967 due to unknown reasons. The A-3's crew went missing. On the next day, Air Wing Eleven lost its first dual-engine RA-5C Vigilante reconnaissance plane of squadron RVAH-13, downed by small-arms fire north and east of Thanh Hoa. The plane's pilot was killed. Lieutenant JG Frank S. Prendergast, the Reconnaissance Attack Navigator (RAN), ejected and was captured. In a bizarre twist, Prendergast shot his captor dead with his survival pistol and was rescued by helicopter.

Two weeks later, on 24 March, an A-6 from VA-85 was downed due to unknown causes with the status of the two-man crew undetermined. Three days later on the 27th, an A-4C of VA-112 disappeared after a strike on a bridge near Vinh. Neither the plane nor its pilot was spotted or recovered. The reason for the loss was never learned.

Completing its scheduled line period, *Kitty Hawk* returned to Subic Bay at the end of March. Even while off-line and away from combat danger, VF-114 was to suffer yet another loss. During training exercises on the 6th of April, an F-4B crashed. Fortunately both crew members ejected successfully without injury.

By mid-April 1967, *Kitty Hawk* was well back in combat off the coast of North Vietnam in the Gulf of Tonkin. On April 24th, during a raid on Kep Airfield north of Hanoi, *Kitty Hawk* and her air wing sustained two losses. An A-6 from VA-85 was shot down near Kep Airfield. The crew members ejected but were captured. On the same day as a result of the same raid, an F-4B from VF-114 flown by Ev Southwick with his RIO, Jimmy Laing, sustained damage from AAA fire to the point that Southwick was unable later to transfer fuel. The F-4B eventually fell victim to fuel starvation. Both crewmen ejected south of Hon Gay and were rescued from the sea by helicopter and returned to *Kitty Hawk*.

Kitty Hawk departed the Gulf of Tonkin on 28 April, returning to action on 8 May. Losses continued. An F-4B from VF-114 was lost immediately after a catapult launch due to over-rotation. One crewman was lost.

Unfortunate as these losses were to the air wing, there were moments of triumph about which the entire ship's company and the air wing could justifiably celebrate.

Air Wing Eleven and *Kitty Hawk* could be proud of VF-114, the Aardvarks and VF-213, the Black Lions. On the 20th of December, one day before the air wing's first loss, the crews of Hugh Dennis (Denny) Wisely and David Jordan, flying an F-4B of VF-114, and David McCrae and David Nichols, also flying an F-4B on loan from VF-114 to VF-213, each shot down a North Vietnamese AN-2 Colt biplane transport aircraft.

In addition to these victories, the first MiG kills of the cruise came from VF-114. Just after being struck by ground fire and prior to their ejection south of Hon Gay due to lack of fuel, Ev Southwick and Jimmy Laing, flying in their F-4B, shot down a MiG-17 on the 24th of April. On the same date, Denny Wisely and Gareth Anderson, flying an F-4B, shot down a MiG-17 that was pursuing Southwick immediately after Southwick and Laing had shot down their MiG.

So by midnight of 13 May 1967, *Kitty Hawk* and Air Wing Eleven had celebrated several victories and experienced many unfortunate mishaps and losses during the cruise. Looming just over the horizon, however, was a bright spot: *Kitty Hawk* and Air Wing Eleven were scheduled to return home soon. In fact, at this time in mid-May 1967, *Kitty Hawk*, Air Wing Eleven, and VF-114 would, in a matter of days, be headed east, out of harm's way, away from the dangers of war to the shores of California. After a long six months at sea, with another month remaining, the combat cruise was about to end.

The duration of carrier deployments to the Gulf of Tonkin, including their transition to and from their home ports, was less than twelve months, averaging probably around seven to eight months per cruise. In general, carriers would stay on their assigned station for about six months, including intervening off-line periods for replenishment and repair. In the larger scheme of life, six to eight months at sea is not a long period of time. But at the start of what would seem an interminable cruise away from family and the safety of home, and in the teeth of combat, it is conceivable that many a sailor or airman would cross off each day, one by one, on a calendar in an inevitable countdown to the time when the cruise would be completed and he could return home.

Jack Rollins had been with VF-114 since *Kitty Hawk* had set sail in November. Ev Southwick had joined the squadron in mid-cruise. Ev and Jack were looking forward to the return as much as anyone.

Chapter 13

May 14, Southeast of Thanh Hoa aboard
Kitty Hawk in the Gulf of Tonkin

AT MIDNIGHT ON SATURDAY, 13 MAY 1967, in the last month of its second six-month combat cruise since the Gulf of Tonkin incident, the USS *Kitty Hawk* remained on station off the coast of North Vietnam. The deck log would record that the warship was in "General Degree of Readiness V." Although the cruise to date had proved grueling and ominously eventful, *Kitty Hawk* continued in a triumphal manner not unlike its ancient ancestors or companion carriers, or for that matter, any other U.S. man-of-war on the high seas.

Kitty Hawk's flight operations for the previous twelve-hour period had just ended and would resume at noon the next day—just twelve hours away. While *Kitty Hawk* stood down, to fill the gap, combat flight operations continued from another carrier on Yankee Station. Although *Kitty Hawk*'s combat operations had temporarily ceased—for twelve hours, at least—some of *Kitty Hawk*'s ship and air wing crew would work throughout the night and into the late morning. Work never really stopped on the big warship.

Kitty Hawk continued to cruise silently through the night in a northeasterly direction at about twelve knots. The prow of the ship parted the surface of the dark sea as the night passed. The white foam, cast to each side of the hull, was momentarily luminous until it faded back and blended into the mysterious waters of the Gulf of Tonkin. The ship had been darkened except for her navigational running lights. Throughout the wee hours until dawn, steaming serenely through the Tonkin Gulf with no apparent operational problems, the ship eventually fell into a relatively quiet calm, catching its breath, as it were, like a bloodied prize fighter waiting for his next round. The balmy wind slid effortlessly across the deck and sliced between the aircraft parked silently aft.

Vigilant though they were, the crew on the navigation bridge relaxed in subdued light and quiet moments. Little conversation occurred among the men as they continued their watch and various duties. Although there were sounds of ship's crewmen working and air wing members performing maintenance on aircraft in the hangar deck, an easy tranquility permeated the cavernous insides of the ship's hull.

Bombs and other ordnance were prepared and positioned, ready for their ascent to the flight deck via the bomb elevators. This and previous days' actions served to confirm that the next day would awake with renewed attacks on North Vietnam.

Deeper in the giant ship, if men were not on watch, they slept. Farther down yet, in the heart of the ship, the monotonous mechanical drone of giant engines and pumps at work could lull to sleep those who were used to the sounds. Throughout the night, various generators and boilers that gave *Kitty Hawk* life had been shut down or taken offline, only to be restarted after awhile. Diverse faint hums and muffled sounds seemed to emanate from the bulkheads, from within the depths of the great ship. Indistinguishable sounds resonated along the faintly lit passageways, the murmur of the giant propellers reverberated throughout the ship, setting up constant vibrations. The crushing sound of seawater cleaved by the mighty warship and the sometimes ghostly creaks of the steel hull belied *Kitty Hawk's* outward, relative peacefulness.

Steaming steadily in the Gulf of Tonkin, *Kitty Hawk* was not without company—she never was. The USS *Carpenter* (DD-825), a Gearing class destroyer, one of several of *Kitty Hawk's* constant companions, sailed in front of her in a sector patrol screen. Like *Kitty Hawk*, she too was darkened.

Sunday, 14 May, dawned with the usual moisture-laden, opaque purplish-blue skies of the South China Sea above the blue waters of the Gulf of Tonkin. *Kitty Hawk's* second watch noted the sunrise in the log book. The slanting sun cast long shadows, created by the stationary aircraft, across the tranquil flight deck. As the sun continued to rise, its rays slid through the scattered clouds low on the eastern horizon, gilding their edges, suffusing the gray steel ship with a yellowish-golden glow. As the sky lightened, the navigational running lights were extinguished. Although *Kitty Hawk* never really slept, this was perhaps the quietest time of the entire day aboard the great ship. During flight operations and immediately before and after, hours were long, the constant work grueling, the stress on the various crews unceasing. Although no one ever got enough rest, the early hours of dawn presented a time when one could reflect and collect one's thoughts and, above all, prepare for the hard day ahead.

But the quiet time was short. *Kitty Hawk*, awakened, was about to spring to life. Members of the ship's company exercised, took walks or short jogs on the flight deck, cleaned passageways, ate breakfast, performed their shipboard routines, made their reports, finished letters home, showered and dressed, tidied up their living areas, perhaps drank a last cup of coffee or smoked a quick cigarette; and went to work.

In parallel fashion, the men of CVW-11, the air wing, had stirred and were also coming to life. The flight and hangar decks, already burdened with aircraft and equipment, became crowded with air wing and ship personnel.

As the round sun started its traverse above the horizon, its horizontal rays mixed with the tropical breeze across the deck, which, perhaps unnoticed by some, soothed many of the crew of *Kitty Hawk* and provided an ambience of respite, a serene beauty that many below could neither see nor appreciate. Now, as the day began, those nocturnal, illusive, but ever-present noises of *Kitty Hawk* were soon replaced or dominated by the collective cacophony associated with aircraft being prepared for attack.

Kitty Hawk continued on as before until about 10:00 hours (10:00 a.m.), when she began a series of maneuvers to change course and speed. Preparations were already underway on the flight deck for the first launch of another day of action against North Vietnam. The war was about to begin anew, as it did each day, for the crews of *Kitty Hawk* and Air Wing Eleven.

Chapter 14
May 14, Northwest of *Kitty Hawk* near Thanh Hoa

AS THE MEN OF *KITTY HAWK* AND AIR WING ELEVEN awoke to a new day at sea on the Gulf of Tonkin on 14 May, a little more than one hundred miles away to the northwest, near Thanh Hoa, so too did brown-faced men and women dressed in camouflage uniforms on the ground in North Vietnam find another new day.

The antiaircraft gun crews, twenty-four hours on duty and twenty-four hours off, had rotated at midnight. Those who were off duty dispersed. They walked many kilometers in total darkness to the safety of tiny huts or small villages, away from the deadly target of Cau Ham Rong. They would return after dark. All during the night, other men and women stirred all around the area. Antiaircraft guns were repaired, replaced, or moved or re-positioned. Men and women with short square shovels dug new emplacements. The batteries were re-supplied with ammunition that had been brought up the Song Ma by boat. Crews worked all night off-loading the awkward boxes and crates and carrying the heavy contents to the various gun emplacements. Carrying the ammunition for the 14.5s and the 37s was relatively easy for one person. Delivering shells for the 57s, 85s and 100s was much more difficult. But the worst was delivering the munitions to the top of Nui Rong and more especially to the top of the much steeper Nui Ngoc.

The boats, parked side by side, their noses nudged into the river bank, had chugged up the Song Ma with their re-supply of munitions. Many boats, their one or two cylinder engines laboring against the fast current of the Song Ma, made two or three deliveries from some point downstream. The motors of each boat continued to run as men and women struggled to offload the cargo. Everyone worked without benefit of light. The boat and off-loading crews knew they were at risk of being discovered by American aircraft and worked furiously. Off-loading from the unsteady boats was tedious and at times dangerous. Some boats had sunk due to the strong current and the heavy loads. At other times, those who off-loaded the munitions would slip and fall off the boats injuring themselves. Or they would slip on the side of the hillocks and fall into some crag or hit their head on a rock outcropping.

During the night, the crews could be seen turning their guns and raising or depressing the barrels as they cleaned the breaches and lubricated the gears and slides. The area was bathed with hushed voices and muted, clanking sounds of tools as people worked on the guns and swabbed the barrels. Sometimes a crew member, acutely punctuating the low drone of noise, would yell at someone in another gun emplacement. Crews ate when they could and smoked often. To hide the small glow of the lit end of a cigarette they would cup their hands over the top of the cigarette. Deep within the ground completely concealed from view, tiny fires cooked rice and fish and heated tea. Few slept but those who did slept next to their guns and only for half an hour.

Another sleepless, humid, hot night passed. The black of tropical darkness retreated into a dull, shadowless gray. On the dim, almost invisible horizon, at the end of the depths of the grayness, where the Song Ma disappeared, the eastern sky turned a faint, deep purple. The dawn was almost broke.

The re-supply boats had long disappeared downstream to hide from the American planes. All was still. Everyone was at their station. No one spoke. All the guns were loaded and readied. Additional shells were positioned strategically around the emplacements. The only sound that could be heard now was the gurgling of the flowing water of the Song Ma as it lapped the shoreline and careened between the rocks and sluiced around the center concrete support pier of Cau Ham Rong.

Night finally relinquished its grip on the landscape and gave way to the dawn marked now by a long sliver of gold that lined the eastern horizon and the edges of low-lying clouds. The Song Ma was tranquil. Reflections began to appear on the sheen of its surface as if to beckon forth the day from its nemesis, the dead of night.

The new day answered the call. A little later, with the sun just above the horizon, its rays slanting over the vibrant green rice paddies and into the fatigued, grainy eyes of Vietnamese men and women who had manned the antiaircraft artillery since midnight, verbal dialogue began to increase. Crew members stretched their limbs and muscles and tried to shake the numbness from their bodies. After their maintenance, the guns were rotated or adjusted, their barrels raised like the wands of so many sorcerers. The defenders of Cau Ham Rong, wide awake now, keenly alert, knew surely they would meet their adversaries again.

Chapter 15
Pre-Briefing for Combat and Manning Aircraft

AT ABOUT NOON ON 14 MAY 1967—Mother's Day—*Kitty Hawk* found herself steaming with the USS *Carpenter* about a hundred fifty miles directly south of Hon Gay, located near Haiphong, and about ninety-two miles east and a little north of Vinh. *Kitty Hawk* was situated halfway, directly east-west, between the coasts of Vietnam and Hainan Island. The entry in the deck log, written in ink beneath a small lamp, pinpointed the position precisely: 18°45'09" N by 107°09'00" E. At this location, the large ship was exactly one hundred eight miles directly southeast of Thanh Hoa City. On this day, about three weeks after his MiG kill, just prior to the day's flight operations, Ev Southwick and his RIO, Jack Rollins, would learn the details of their first combat mission for the day.

Late that morning, flight leaders of Air Wing Eleven received their briefing for the upcoming mission in the Strike Operations Center and then returned to their respective ready rooms to await launch time. Their mission was to destroy warehouses in the Hai Phong harbor area. It was an "alpha strike," the term used when it is the first strike on a target involving the entire air wing.

To some, the ready room was home away from home, the hub of many activities for members of the squadron. Pilots, RIOs, and Bombardier Navigators (BNs) loitered around, drank coffee, exchanged stories, and analyzed past missions here. The ready room served as an entertainment center, a place to socialize, fraternize, and relax; and a place to prepare for the missions ahead. Even if not involved in a particular mission, aircrews often hung around the ready room. They gravitated to the ready room even when there was no compelling reason to do so.

The mission, however, was changed. Instead of hearing the anticipated *"Pilots, man your aircraft"* for the planned strike, the seated Navy airmen in the Aardvarks' ready room as well as the men in the other squadrons were informed of a new target. They were briefed about altitudes, headings, type of ordnance, radio frequencies, launch time, and other particulars that would be needed for a successful launch, attack, and recovery. Upon hearing the details for the strike on the new target, a slight murmur arose from the congregation of seated combat pilots and radar intercept officers. The morning routine hours gave way to anticipation as the aircrews prepared for their new flight mission.

The men of VF-114 had just learned that Air Wing Eleven would attack the Thanh Hoa Bridge—the same bridge that the Vietnamese had named the Ham Rong Bridge—northwest of Thanh Hoa in Route Package IV. This prickly target superseded the now-scrubbed mission against the warehouses in Hai Phong.

The mission against the Thanh Hoa Bridge would include multiple, coordinated strikes of A-4 Skyhawks from VA-112 and VA-144 and larger A-6 Intruder attack planes from VA-85. In all, about twenty-five aircraft would be used for the strike. Other aircraft—tankers, helicopters, and reconnaissance planes—would be used to support the strike but would not participate in the attack. All strike and support aircraft for this mission would originate from Air Wing Eleven, from *Kitty Hawk*. Together, they would form an incredible force.

Heavily laden with bombs, the attack planes would be highly vulnerable to antiaircraft fire, or what was commonly called "flak." Once committed to the bombing run, the A-4s and A-6s could not deviate from the flight path, lest the ordnance miss its mark. They would be easy targets for barrage fire from the triple-A guns. Hence, if the antiaircraft air defenses of the North Vietnamese could be suppressed, taken out altogether, the attack planes would likely complete their mission successfully. The risk to American attack planes and their pilots would be greatly reduced. F-4 Phantoms from VF-114 were assigned the role of flak suppression.

The Thanh Hoa Bridge had been attacked many times before. A formidable target, it had sustained damage but not been destroyed. Many American planes had been damaged and quite a few shot down during previous attacks on the bridge. With its heavy air defenses and past history of attacks, it could only be assumed that the area around the Thanh Hoa Bridge would awake with a vengeance.

Like the briefing for the mission given to VF-114 in their ready room, other similar briefings were being given simultaneously in the ready rooms of the other squadrons. The only squadron of Air Wing Eleven not involved in the strike mission that day was VF-213, the other F-4 squadron.

Ev Southwick, with RIO Jack Rollins seated behind him in their F-4 Phantom II, would lead the flak suppression strike of three F-4s in support of their strike mission. All three F-4s in their flight would be armed with Zuni rockets that would be unleashed on the enemy. The other two F-4s would be flown by Wayne Miller and George Stock; and Phil Brown and Jim Cook.

The F-4 flak suppression mission would arrive on target in the area of the Thanh Hoa Bridge from the north, while the A-4 and A-6 bombers would arrive on target not more than twenty seconds later from the south. The F-4s would be clear of the target area just as the A-4s and A-6s began their diving attack. The overall strike was designed with surprise and diversion in mind. Coordinated attacks from opposite directions would cause confusion among the North Vietnamese air defenses. The F-4s' flak suppression mission against the Thanh Hoa Bridge's air defenses would initiate the confusion. This would allow for the destruction of the bridge by the A-4s and A-6s.

Because of the demands of previous combat and other operations, the pilots flew whatever aircraft was available within the squadron for any given mission. Ev and Jack and the F-4 Phantom they were slated to fly, with the number "201" painted on each side of the aircraft beneath and a little forward of the cockpit, would have the call sign "Linfield Two Zero One." Within the flight, their call sign would be simply "Lin One." Also painted on each side of the fuselage near the tail in bold block numerals was the last four digits of the six digit bureau number "3001."

Prior to and concurrent with the pilot's briefing, on the flight deck of *Kitty Hawk*, the Plane Captain and a small crew were busy preparing Ev and Jack's F-4—Linfield Two Zero One—for the mission. When not in flight, each aircraft was managed by a Plane Captain, dressed in a brown jersey—a Brown Shirt, as he was (is) called—who oversees all maintenance for that particular aircraft and who was responsible for it when it was not in flight. The Plane Captain performed preflight checks prior to the pilot and RIO entering the aircraft. Among the many tasks the Plane Captain had to complete, he checked for damage, leaks, loose panels, and unsecured doors; that the tailhook up-lock was removed; that the tires and landing gears were in operational condition and ready for the mission. He checked the conditions of the stabilators, ailerons, speed brakes, and rudder; he checked for obstructions that might be in the air intakes, that the pitot and static system ports were clear. He checked that the fuel dump masts, located at the very back of the plane and aft of each wing, were unobstructed. He checked various lights and many other features of the plane.

Ev and Jack's F-4 sat among other F-4s, A-4s, and A-6s aft of the island and slightly askew on the deck. Loaded with fuel and ordnance and with heavy chains attached to secure the plane to the flight deck and chocks securing the wheels, Linfield Two Zero One and its Plane Captain awaited the Phantom's flight crew.

Finally the order, anticipated earlier, was given: "*Pilots, man your aircraft!*" The announcement came from the air officer, or "Air Boss," located at the top of the island on the level known as primary-flight or more simply "pri-fly." This was the definitive signal for all pilots, RIOs, and BNs to go to their respective aircraft. The instruction sounded in the ready rooms through small speakers and across the flight deck from powerful loudspeakers mounted high above on the island.

Having received news of the target and the mission plans during the preflight briefing in the various ready rooms, the pilots and aircrews for about thirty planes made their way to the open expanse of the flight deck. The flight deck was abuzz with activity as the planes, huddled toward the rear of the ship in what is referred to as *the pack,* were surrounded by members of each squadron and men dressed in colorful jerseys.

The flight deck crew had already performed what is referred to as the "FOD walk down" or more simply, the walk down. The purpose of the walk down is to spot and pick up any foreign object debris—hence FOD—from the flight deck that could be sucked into the jet engines.

The F-4s, A-4s, and A-6s, spotted aft of the catapults, were arranged in a manner that would allow for systematic, sequential, and simultaneous launching. After the auxiliary aircraft were launched, for this mission the Phantoms were scheduled to be launched next, before the A-4 and A-6 bombers, and therefore sat near the lead of the pack nearest the catapults but still aft of the island.

Beneath the flight deck, the boilers and steam generators were operating at their fullest capacity to provide constantly renewable steam pressure for the two bow and two waist catapults. The four catapults, with whiffs of steam rising from their tracks and wafting a short distance back, were ready to launch the strike mission.

Mixed in with the noise of planes being readied and crew members talking loudly, the loudspeakers continued with a litany of instructions and reminders from the Air Boss. As men worked on the flight deck and pilots walked to their aircraft, the loudspeakers blared out:

"Attention on the flight deck: Pilots are manning up for the thirteen-thirty [13:30 hours] launch. Get into complete flight deck uniform—shirts on and sleeves rolled down, helmets on, chin strap fastened, goggles down, float coats on and fastened. Check for all loose gear about the deck."

The "F" or Foxtrot flag, a square white flag with a red square turned forty-five degrees within the white field, was raised on a halyard to the dip (part way to the top) on top of the island, a visual indication that flight operations were imminent.

Everywhere among the assembled planes—the F-4s, A-4s, A-6s, and the auxiliary aircraft—the aircrews performed checks and began to climb aboard their aircraft. Like so many ants around a small dead animal, men were around, next to, beneath, and now climbing on each aircraft.

Along with the pilots and RIOs of VF-114 and aircrew of the other squadrons, Ev emerged from the catwalk wearing his flight suit and G-suit and walked aft, toward the rear of the flat, sprawling flight deck of *Kitty Hawk*. He wore an emergency survival vest over his flight suit that contained a pistol, UHF radio, flashlight, and other survival-related items. Ev carried his helmet and charts in his hands. Passing the superstructure of the island to his left, on the side of which were painted, in white, two large numerals, "63," the arresting cables at his feet, and the waist catapults, Ev walked toward his waiting Phantom.

Jack was late arriving on the flight deck. He was trying to find a Purple Heart medal for a squadron mate. Several days after *Kitty Hawk* had returned to line duty, an F-4 on a reconnaissance mission received small arms fire and a crew member was wounded. He was scheduled to leave *Kitty Hawk* on the COD (carrier onboard delivery) twin-engine, turbo-prop plane that day—in fact, just before the mission now against the Thanh Hoa Bridge. After scouring around, unable to locate a Purple Heart medal, Jack gave up his search. He made his way to the COD to tell his comrade he could not find a Purple Heart for him and to wish him luck. Then Jack made his way to his F-4 to join Ev.

Both men conversed with the Plane Captain and performed their own visual preflight inspection as they walked around their F-4. They checked for loose panels, ordnance loading, leaks—anything that may grab their attention or any anomalies that may be discovered. The area around them was congested with planes and people in colorful jerseys, all talking, and other aircrews performing in the same manner.

Pilots and aircrew are only part of the equation of flight operations on board an aircraft carrier. While the pilots represent the vanguard of the air wing, it's the flight-deck crew, wearing a variety of colors, who manage the planes and direct the pilots to the point of launch. The choreography of flight operations is coordinated through the colors of the jerseys. Each color designates a specific function to be performed in concert with many other concurrent activities that occur during a launch sequence.

Plane directors, because of their yellow jerseys, are referred to as "Yellow Shirts" and are the most visible on the flight deck. There are usually six to eight Yellow Shirts on the flight deck of a carrier. The Yellow Shirts hold a highly respected and prestigious position in U.S. naval aviation. At the top of flight operations' organizational pyramid, the Yellow Shirts are the heartbeat of the flight deck. They control movement of all aircraft and initiate the launch sequence. The catapult and arresting-gear officer, the flight deck officer, and the Air Boss each wear the yellow jersey.

In addition to the brown shirt of the Plane Captain and the yellow jerseys of the plane directors, there are purple, blue, green, white and red shirts. To the untrained eye, viewing flight-deck operations may seem confusing, but each man, identified by the color of his jersey, has a specific duty. There is no confusion.

The Purple Shirts are responsible for refueling aircraft. Blue Shirts provide specialized plane handling requirements and are responsible for placing and removing the chocks. Green Shirts have a multitude of responsibilities including maintaining and operating the catapult and arresting-gear equipment. White Shirts provide quality control, safety, and, when designated with a red cross on their jerseys, medical services. Red Shirts, actually a combination of air wing personnel and ship's company, are ordnancemen and crash and salvage crews. They are also responsible for ordnance disposal.

During flight operations, if one is not wearing one of the above colors, he is not on the flight deck.

The men on the flight deck may have different functions denoted by the color of their shirts but they all have one thing in common: safety. They all wear goggles, gloves, and protective head gear with sound attenuating ear protectors that protrude from each side of their head. Some wear kneepads.

Ev and Jack's Phantom, Linfield Two Zero One, sat ready with the outer tips of its wings folded and with the forward and aft canopies raised in anticipation of the fighter jet's occupants. The Phantom, with a white aardvark inset within an orange stripe at the top of the vertical stabilizer, had already been loaded with Zuni rockets in their long, cylindrical rocket pods beneath each wing. The internal fuel tanks, situated just above the engines and contained within the wings of their F-4, had also been fully fueled. To augment the fuel capacity, as was the custom, a large, bullet-like fuel tank was attached to the plane's belly along the centerline. Placed in their recesses beneath the fuselage of the aircraft and immediately to each side of the centerline fuel tank, Sparrow missiles would provide the Phantom with its own air defense capabilities.

Assisted by the crew, Ev began to climb up onto the F-4 from the port side of the aircraft using the aluminum ladder, located just in front of the left air intake and intake ramps, extendable from the bottom of the fuselage, and the staggered foot holes recessed on the side of the fuselage that serve as steps. It's important for the airmen to ascend the short aluminum ladder and footholes with the correct foot sequencing; otherwise, the pilot's or RIO's legs become crossed up at the top, making the last step up difficult.

Ev climbed into the Phantom first. As he climbed the ladder and the foot holes, his body passed the thin red stripes painted on the side of the fuselage that formed a horizontal V and the words that warned "JET INTAKE." From the top foot hole, Ev pulled himself up by grabbing the top of the leading edge of the fixed intake ramp with his right hand and then the rear of the front fixed canopy with his left. Once on top, he steadied himself. In one fluid motion, but being careful to straddle the control stick with his feet and to miss the various controls and switches located on the left and right consoles, with his hands firmly grasping the edge of the fixed canopy and steadying himself to each side, Ev stepped into the front cockpit and lowered himself into the pilot's seat.

The Plane Captain followed Ev and helped him with his strap-in preparations. Ev connected his oxygen and communication lines. He turned the oxygen selector switch to *on* and checked that there was normal flow of oxygen—so that he could breathe normally.

Then Ev reached down and secured the lower leg restraints that would keep his feet in a tight position if for some reason he had to eject. Finally, he began to buckle himself into the seat, using the hip and shoulder rings and quick-release fittings that would secure his body tightly in place.

The Plane Captain pulled a pin on the ejection seat, thereby arming it. He showed the pin to Ev to alert him that the ejection seat was now armed and could be fired. Ev acknowledged the signal.

Climbing into the rear seat of the cockpit required the same agility and initial maneuvers up the ladder and foot holes. But because the foot holes are positioned beneath the front cockpit, the RIO's entry to his cockpit required more movement. Jack followed Ev up the same ladder and foot holes a few minutes later. He walked along the fuselage and canopy rail to the back seat of the Phantom. Having propped his right leg up on top of the port intake to steady his stance, he turned left, took hold of the front of the rear canopy, stepped down into the rear cockpit, and lowered himself into the seat.

The Plane Captain assisted Jack with his preparations and his buckling in. Just as he had with Ev, he armed the ejection seat and confirmed this to Jack who acknowledged that his ejection seat could be fired.

Satisfied that the two occupants were correctly strapped in and all was ready for them, the Plane Captain descended the ladder and retracted it back into the recess at the bottom just at the side of the F-4's fuselage.

Settled into the back seat, Jack extended his right hand and adjusted his altimeter to the correct barometric pressure and altitude. The altimeter read "75 feet," the height of *Kitty Hawk*'s flight deck above the water. He made sure that the TACAN (tactical air navigation system) and UHF (ultra high frequency) radio and other switches were all in the *off* position. Jack checked that the manual canopy unlock switch was in the forward position and that the various circuit breakers and other switches were set correctly.

The items that Ev had to check in the pilot's cockpit prior to starting engines were numerous. Some of these included: generator switches in the *off* position, oxygen supply, height of the seat, position of the rudder pedals, the stick grip was secure, all circuit breakers were in, gear handle down, ordnance arming switches *off*, fuel dump switches *off*, weapons selector switch *off*, instrument panel and cockpit lights *off*, and radar altimeter *off*.

Elsewhere on the flight deck, around the two airmen, now seated in their Phantom, the same scenario was more or less replicated for all of the other aircraft as pilots, RIOs and BNs manned their flying war machines and the ground crews prepared them for combat. Other plane captains and crew thronged around the armed aircraft.

The Yellow Shirts, having already donned their protective gear, waited for their time to commence their plane directing activities. High in the island in pri-fly, other men performed their duties as well in preparation of the launch. Radars rotated on top of the island. The large ship swayed and the men on the deck could feel the swaying motion and the slight dip to each side as the ship rolled slightly with the sea. The wind over the deck blew in everyone's face as it whistled in and around the combat aircraft.

Inside the front and aft cockpits of Linfield Two Zero One, Ev and Jack continued to prepare for the mission, The front and aft cockpits of the F-4 Phantom are not tiny but they're not spacious either. There is no wasted space inside. Each cockpit, measuring less than three feet from left to right (side to side), or from front to back (from the instrument panel to the seat), is packed with a complicated and congested array of dials, knobs and switches. The close proximity of levers, protruding handles, buttons, consoles, lights and panels, all connote utility of function and specific purpose. Immediately facing each airman, multiple glass-covered, black-faced, round gauges with white pointers (needles) and white numbers around the circumference of the dials, display a wide range of diverse unrelated and interrelated data. Unlike the dashboard of an automobile, the plane's instrument panels and associated consoles are unadorned with frills. Any person's first gaze at the cockpits of an F-4 would result in awe if not total bewilderment as to what he was seeing. Without knowledge and understanding of the instruments and the information they provide, it may seem as if each instrument or handle or switch has been crammed together in a disorganized or arbitrary manner. In such close quarters, space for all the gauges and levers and switches is scarce. Even though each instrument competes for display space and visibility, a logic behind the positioning of the various instruments and gauges does prevail—even though some instruments are less visible than others and some levers or handles are less convenient that the rest. Such are the features and complex characteristics that reside within the intricate confines of the F-4 Phantom II's front and back cockpits.

Although there are a myriad of instruments in the pilot's cockpit, their exact positions varying slightly among different versions of the F-4, three instruments dominate the pilot's visual environment. Situated directly in front of the pilot, these include, from top down, the radar scope (about five inches in diameter); the Attitude Director Indicator (ADI), known in civilian parlance as the "artificial horizon;" and immediately below that, the Horizontal Situation Indicator (HSI), or "gyro-compass," as it is called by general aviation enthusiasts. The rate of climb or descent indicator and the altimeter are found just to the right of the three larger instruments; the airspeed indicator is located just to the left. Various hydraulic, oil, and pneumatic pressure gauges are located on a console just below the main instrument panel, within easy reach of the pilot. Flight control gauges, the fuel control panel, and levers that operate the flaps, landing gears, throttles, and weapons systems are on the left console. The right console contains the wing fold control panel and other functions associated with internal management of cockpit and ancillary systems.

Immediately to the right of the main instrument panel, containing the radar scope, ADI and HSI, are two vertical columns of four instruments. Each instrument measures two inches in diameter. These provide information about the health of the power plants—the engines, the heart of the aircraft. Set side by side from top down, with the left and right columns corresponding with the port and starboard engines, the first instrument encountered at the top is the fuel flow gauge, which measures the flow of fuel in thousands of pounds per hour. The second gauge is the tachometer, which registers revolutions per minute (rpm) but as a percentage of maximum rpm as opposed to actual rpm themselves. The third gauge down the column displays the temperature of the exhaust gases in degrees Centigrade. The last, or bottom, of the four gauges registers the open or closed position of the nozzle at the extreme aft end of the engine. The nozzle, commonly referred to as "turkey feathers," is comprised of circumferentially articulated fan-like protrusions that open and close annularly, depending on the power being produced, thereby increasing or decreasing the diameter, or cross-sectional area of the exhaust outlet. The nozzle position instrument indicates that the nozzles are closed or open or somewhere in between; but in fact, while the nozzles may open to their widest circumference and close to their narrowest circumference, they never completely seal off the exhaust opening. Immediately above the left vertical column for the port engine instruments, a fifth instrument indicates fuel quantity.

The arresting or tailhook control handle is located immediately to the right of the engine instruments. The tailhook would be tested; that is, lowered, and then retracted prior to launch. Of course, the tailhook, used to arrest the forward movement of the Phantom at recovery, would play an absolutely essential role when the Phantom returned to *Kitty Hawk.*

The aft cockpit, from which the forward view is limited, contains the same flight and navigational instruments as the front cockpit but is dominated mostly by an enshrouded, or hooded, radar scope that the RIO extends up so he can better read the scope. The RIO does not have visual access to a second set of engine instruments or, for that matter, any throttle or flight controls. It is not possible to fly the Navy F-4 from the back seat.

Now, with Ev and Jack securely buckled in their cockpits and finally with the initial front and backseat checklists completed, both men put on and secured their helmets. Like the airmen situating themselves in the other planes around them, both Ev and Jack continued with their respective pre-flight checks.

Ev set his altimeter to "75 feet," just as Jack had.

A small square cart—the starting cart—sat next to Linfield Two Zero One. Once started, the cart would provide electrical power and compressed air for the engines, one engine at a time. It was the Brown Shirt's duty to attach the hoses and electrical cables from the cart to the belly of the Phantom.

There is little room beneath the wings and fuselage around which to maneuver. Due to the tight geometry defined by the large centerline fuel tank, the Sparrow missiles in their recesses, the load of Zuni rockets—two clusters of long pods, each containing four rockets, beneath each wing—and the angularity of the wings and, of course, the extended main landing gears, working space is cramped. Making the electrical and air hose connections beneath the Phantom necessitates focus and agility. The constricted space beneath the aircraft requires the men to work in a low crouch or kneeling position. If something went wrong, escape would be possible but not immediate.

The air hose would provide a rush of air from the compressor in the starting cart to the starter motors of each engine to begin spinning the engine's compressor and turbine shaft. Electrical cables from the cart provide external electrical power until the Phantom's generators could fulfill that role.

Ev and Jack, now seated in their respective cockpits, the sun glinting through the open canopies, waited for the command to start the F-4's engines and to move the fully loaded Phantom toward the catapults.

Chapter 16
Launch from *Kitty Hawk*

AN OVERPOWERING VOICE EMANATED FROM *PRI-FLY* on top of the island high above the flight deck of *Kitty Hawk*. Its solitary instruction from giant loudspeakers reverberated across the flight deck with a truncated echo and for a brief moment dominated all other sounds. This would be the last verbal command given, its message clear: "*Pilots, start your engines!*"

Kitty Hawk had turned into the wind and steadied on its "foxtrot corpen," defined as the course on which flight operations would be conducted. This maneuver provided optimum wind across the deck (bow to stern) and facilitated the launch of aircraft. This maneuver, combined with the ship's increased speed, usually resulted in a twenty-five- to thirty-knot wind across the deck. The deck and launch crew proceeded through their intense preparations to launch the aircraft that were still tightly packed aft of the island.

The engine in the starter cart positioned to the left of Linfield Two Zero One started with a howl. The starter cart's engine, air compressor and generator eventually rose to operating levels.

Ev selected external power by placing the generator toggle switch, located on the generator control panel to his right, to the external position. He continued to scan the flight instrument panel, noting the needles of each gauge and making sure that the external power source had reached its rated voltage and frequency.

The external electrical power provided by the starting cart would power up the electrical systems in the same manner as would the onboard generators. Various dials and gauges and lights instantly came to life. The whirring sound of the gyro motor and various pumps, which might be faintly heard in the absence of any other noise, was drowned out by the din of the starter cart and muted by Ev's helmet. Ev watched as the needles of various gauges danced and then stabilized, and various lights revealed the status of the multiple aircraft systems. He checked the systems' warning lights, missile status, and fire warning lights, as well as fuel quantity, the flap position indicator, landing gear indicator, and pump pressure gauges.

Visual confirmation through the instruments is of paramount importance but sounds are also telltale indicators. Often it is the absence of familiar sounds or the intrusion of unfamiliar noises that signal something is not right. Ev listened for aural tones and paid close attention to any sounds that may indicate any anomaly with the F-4's systems.

Ev, continuing with his checks, noted the position of the inlet ramps and speed brakes, and peered at the weapons sight (pipper) on the top of the console, knowing it would need to be set for firing air-to-ground rockets. While other instruments were activated, the aircraft engine instruments had not yet come to life.

Ev and Jack selected radio and navigational frequencies, and finally set their clocks. They were ready to start the engines. Not more than ten minutes had elapsed from the time they had climbed into their cockpits.

The Plane Captain, his hands in the air, stood in front of and a little to one side of the Phantom so that Ev had a clear view of him. Then with his right forearm and hand bent at the elbow and his fingers making a circular motion next to his head, his left hand extended straight, the Plane Captain indicated that the starboard engine was to be started first.

Ev acknowledged this signal. He confirmed that the engine start switch located next to the throttles pointed to the right engine. This would allow air to flow to the starboard engine from the starter cart. Ev made sure that the engine master switch for the starboard engine, located also just to the right of the throttles on his left, was turned on. The engine master switch directs power to the fuel boost and transfer pumps.

The starting cart, now running at full rpm, blew air through the air hose to the air turbine starter that would begin spinning the compressor and turbine blade shaft on the starboard engine. As the engine began to spool up, Ev scanned the vertical row of instruments for the starboard engine again. During operations, each instrument provides precise and independent information. Collectively, when read together, the information from these four instruments presents a direct indication of the status of each engine. At this moment, however, other than for the tachometer, there was not yet any activity for the other engine instruments to record.

With the compressor and turbine blades of the starboard engine turning, the right tachometer immediately registered, its needle slowly rotating to the right. When Ev noted that the needle was pointing to a little more than ten percent, the first numerical interval on the small circular dial, he advanced the right throttle with his left hand halfway up the quadrant past the idle détente and then back to idle. He monitored the fuel flow.

The right throttle allowed a small controlled flow of atomized fuel and air into a section of the combustion chamber. Ev depressed the ignition button on the front of the right throttle thereby causing an electrical spark, much like that of a sparkplug in a car, to arc in one of the subchambers of the engine's combustion chamber. The electrical arc ignited the fuel-air mixture. The contained, subdued explosion that resulted was not felt by either airman. Because of the cross-fire tubes leading into the remaining subchambers, soon the entire combustion chamber was alight with fire. The needle of the temperature gauge, located just below the tachometer, jumped immediately as the fuel ignited. The engine came alive with a continuous, muffled, moaning roar.

Ev remained vigilant about the exhaust gas temperature and ensured that the heat did not rise above specified ranges or for longer than specified durations. He watched further as the tachometer and fuel flow gauges were registering the ignition. Fuel flow, in pounds per hour, registered in the normal range while the rpm rose predictably. Ev heard the drone of the engine spooling up. Satisfied from a visual survey of his instruments that he had sustained ignition, he released the ignition button. While Ev continued to monitor the instruments, the engine continued to spool up. The tachometer showed an increase in rpm as the gauge's needle continued its clockwise spin.

The engine spooled up and, at a little less than 60 percent, the generator came on line. The F-4 was now electrically independent. Ev listened and watched as the engine spooled to 65 percent. Now all engine instruments in the right column were registering continuous and stable data about fuel flow, rpm and temperature. All operational aspects for the starboard engine were in the normal range. With a thumbs-up, Ev signaled to the Plane Captain that he could turn his attention to starting the port engine.

The Plane Captain, still standing in front of the F-4, with the fingers of his left hand making a circular motion next to his head, his right hand extended, signaled to Ev to start the port engine. Again, Ev acknowledged this signal.

By moving the small switch on the engine start panel beneath the throttles to the "L," or left, position, Ev allowed compressed air from the starter cart to transfer to the port engine. He moved the toggle of the engine master switch for the port engine to the *on* position. He was ready now to start the port engine, Ev followed the same routine as he had for the starboard engine.

Now with both engines at 65 percent rpm, Ev scanned the instrument panel again for any incongruency. Both engines and both generators on the Phantom were running satisfactorily.

By pointing with the finger of his right hand to the palm of his left hand and then pulling it away, Ev indicated that the Plane Captain could disconnect the air hose and the electrical cables from beneath the Phantom. The Plane Captain responded with the same signal. The air hose and electrical cables were detached from the belly of the Phantom and the panel doors secured. The F-4 was completely self-sustaining.

Ev and Jack both activated levers located to their left, causing their canopies to close. Instantly their world became constrained to that of swelling heat, muted noises, and odors redolent of various fabrics and metal, hydraulic fluid, and sweat—in all, the unique, typical, and unmistakable smell of an enclosed cockpit of a military fighter jet. The canopies were secured and sealed. The sky that had been open above them was now separated from the airmen by the clear, hardened plastic of the canopies just inches over their heads. While the wind continued to swirl around the Phantom, the air inside the enclosed capsule fell suddenly still and, with the temperature on the rise, became muggy.

Having made the transition from the large, open-air flight deck of an aircraft carrier, seemingly with lots of space around them, both men now found themselves, as they had many times before, in a tight, self-contained, highly specialized, technologically oriented, rarefied environment.

Simultaneously around them, the same preflight and starting procedures were more or less repeated for each aircraft.

Inside their planes, with helmets on and canopies lowered and secured, flight crews could only vaguely hear the transient whining sounds of various pumps and motors, gyros and valves, and the deep, continuous, resonating sound of their engines' compressors and turbines, and the more muted sounds of the jet engines of the surrounding aircraft.

Outside the planes, the shrill, roaring sound of the jet engines of at least thirty strike and support aircraft shrieked across the flight deck of *Kitty*

Hawk. The flight deck was awash with high-pitched noises of turbines winding up and the thundering, overpowering roar of jet exhaust.

Life on the flight deck of any aircraft carrier is precarious but during flight operations, it's dangerous. As the planes on *Kitty Hawk* would move to the catapults for launch, things would become even more intense, the danger level would heighten. The slightest misstep could spell disaster.

In an environment free of any noise or externally dominant attribute, when a person's senses are registering information equally, a person's reactions take into account all external forces and his senses provide a safe course of action. Let one attribute—very bright light, a horrific odor, a hot flame—become dominant, the sense that registers it will prevail over the others. On a flight deck, the high pitched, piercing sound of turbines and the violent roar of exhaust dominate everything. With sound all around, it is difficult for the hearing sense to sort out, mark, and position any one sound. For all sound is now blurred. Dangers on a flight deck still lurk, as they always have, but the danger level is now exacerbated and amplified by the dominating sound. Losing one's awareness of one's surroundings and near proximities can be fatal. Arresting cables can trip; taxiing planes can collide or strike those who may be unaware of their movement; a person could become geographically disoriented due to the constant noise, commotion and movement of planes and people and, however slight, the rolling or pitching of the carrier itself. Then, most perilous of all, whirling propellers and rotor blades of the propeller driven aircraft and helicopters can chew up a person and cut him to ribbons in less than a second. There is the instantaneous suction of the jet engines at the air intakes and the hyper-heat and high velocity of the hot exhaust gases out the back. People have been sucked into a jet intake or blown overboard by the exhaust. Keeping one's head about oneself is paramount during flight operations. More than ever, it is necessary to pay attention. But those who work on a flight deck are professionals, acutely aware of all dangers. They know how to obviate them. They are experts at danger management.

Now, with the electrical systems of Ev and Jack's Phantom no longer dependent on outside power sources, all other instruments found before Ev in the front seat and Jack in the back began to register data. Both airmen continued through their respective post-start, preflight checklists. Radios and TACAN were switched on. By pulling on a small round knob at the base of their ADIs, Ev and Jack caused the horizon needle on the blue dial to set properly. Thus they had "caged" each ADI. They watched as the artificial horizon and other pointers settled into position.

The Plane Captain indicated to Ev to test the control surfaces. Moving the control stick with his gloved right hand, Ev tested the stabilators and ailerons. He tested the rudder as he moved the rudder pedals beneath his feet. The Green Shirts monitored the movement of the control surfaces. Under the watchful eye of the Plane Captain, and with his instructions, Ev extended and retracted the refueling probe on the starboard side of the plane, popped out and retracted the ram air turbine (RAT) on the port side of the fuselage, and dropped and raised the tailhook.

The F-4 and its systems were operating satisfactorily. Ev and Jack were ready for flight. The Phantom, with call sign Linfield Two Zero One, armed and fully fueled, with its crew on board, was prepared for the flak suppression mission against the air defenses of the Thanh Hoa Bridge.

Each Yellow Shirt is assigned a sector on the flight deck during flight operations. The first Plane Director is responsible for moving the planes out of their parking spots and into the flow of traffic toward the catapults. With both hands over his head and his thumbs pointing to the outside, the Plane Director signaled the chocks were to be withdrawn from the wheels and the tie-down chains removed from beneath the plane. Blue Shirts removed the chocks from the landing gears. The Plane Captain removed the heavy chains that secured the plane to the flight deck.

Standing in full view of Ev, the Plane Captain held the chains at eye level and then placed them over his shoulders and saluted Ev to show him that the chains had been removed, that the F-4 was no longer constrained from movement. Ev acknowledged this action. Although this last acknowledgement essentially ended the Plane Captain's role until the plane returned, he would walk with the plane, chains over his shoulder, as it was directed to the catapult by the Yellow Shirts. If needed, if the process were to be aborted, the Plane Captain would be ready to tie the plane down again to any one or several of the thousand tie-down locations that are located on a grid every six feet or so across the entire flight deck.

Ev's eyes were glued to the Yellow Shirt in front of him. The man in yellow raised his hands to each side to eye level and, with a cross-wise motion of his forearms and hands, indicated to Ev to move his Phantom forward. Ev acknowledged the instruction and eased the throttles forward with his left hand. He tapped the rudder pedals to test the brakes' responsiveness while simultaneously moving, rotating the control stick—"wiping the cock-pit" as it's called—to test the flight controls. The rudder, stabilators, and ailerons waggled in response to his commands.

Given the fact that the inertia of a fully loaded plane is greater than that for a plane without ordnance, movement of a loaded aircraft must be more gradual. Applying too much throttle will result in the plane being unable to stop in the same distance it would if it were lightly loaded. As a general rule, prior to launching, throttle settings on board the carrier do not exceed about 65 to 75 percent. More throttle than that could cause damage—deck crew members could be sucked into the intakes or blown overboard by the exhaust. Hence, proper throttle control is essential and carefully managed by the pilot.

The Plane Director handed Ev off to another Yellow Shirt using an exaggerated transfer signal—pointing fingers and both arms directly at the new Plane Director. Ev acknowledged the transfer. The Plane Captain still walked alongside the Phantom.

Other F-4s, on their way to the catapults, moved in sequence behind Ev and Jack. With their exhaust roaring and their compressors and turbines whining, aircraft for the strike were being stacked up behind each catapult in anticipation of launch.

The pilot of the rescue helicopter, situated toward the bow of *Kitty Hawk*, its engines and rotors already operating at idle, turned the throttle on the collective, a lever to his left that controls the pitch of the main rotor blades, to full rpm. The giant overhead rotor and tail rotor spun up to full speed. The pilot pulled up on the collective with his left hand to increase lift. The weight of the helicopter was being transferred to the large rotor blades. The pilot maintained control of the aircraft with the tail rotor pedals and the cyclic, a control stick found between his knees. The rescue helicopter lifted off *Kitty Hawk*'s deck and was the first launch of the mission.

The Foxtrot flag was raised close up (to the top) and flew high above the island. This was the indication that flight operations aboard *Kitty Hawk* had begun. The Foxtrot flag would not be lowered and stowed until after the last aircraft had recovered aboard *Kitty Hawk*.

The E-2 Hawkeye launched next. The tanker aircraft, and then the planes that flew various Combat Aerial Patrols, or CAPs, that were intended to protect the ship, would follow.

While Ev and Jack performed their run-up, and as they taxied, other air-craft—in addition to the aircraft that had taken off in support of the mission, as well as the COD—also inched their way to the catapults.

A typical launch cycle is one plane every sixty seconds per catapult. Aircraft cannot be launched simultaneously from both waist catapults or from both bow catapults. Two planes can take off simultaneously, however, if one is launched from the starboard waist catapult and the other from the port bow catapult.

To steer the F-4 on the flight deck, Ev depressed a button on the control stick that allowed him to turn the Phantom's nose landing gear left or right through the use of the rudder pedals. As Ev maneuvered Linfield Two Zero One closer to the catapults, the Phantom passed over the arresting cables, which during recovery would be elevated mere inches above the flight deck and supported by what were called "fiddle bridges," but which now lay flush with the steel plating.

He was following an A-3 tanker, the largest and heaviest plane on *Kitty Hawk*. The A-3 was finally positioned on the catapult. The jet blast deflector rose behind it.

Being next in line, Ev's time for the catapult was about to arrive. He moved his left hand to the flap control panel next to the left console and activated a small lever to lower the flaps that were located inboard at the back of the main wings. Following instructions from the plane director, Ev maneuvered his F-4 into position behind the jet blast deflector of the port waist catapult and waited for the A-3 on the catapult in front of him to be launched. He did not have long to wait.

The Yellow Shirt finally gave the instruction to Ev (by holding his arms straight out to either side) to unfold the F-4's wingtips.

Ev reached for the wing fold control panel on his right and activated the wing fold system. With another signal from the Plane Director that consisted of the palm of his left hand hitting the bent elbow of the right arm, Ev locked the wingtips into their slightly upturned position.

The roar from the twin engines of the A-3 tanker that had been positioned on the catapult filled the air as hot exhaust gases were blown vertically up by the shield just aft of the A-3 and in front of Ev and Jack. The A-3 was blasted down the catapult track and was now free of the ship. The jet blast deflector immediately lowered, and the shuttle retracted.

Steam rose from the catapult track that led obliquely from the centerline of the giant ship to the edge of the angled deck and the expanse of the sea. Ev saw, in the wafting, escaping steam, another solitary Yellow Shirt standing astride the catapult track with his arms raised. This solo person, called the "Spotter," standing alone, bug-eyed with his goggles, odd-looking with his ear protectors prominently protruding from each side of his head, was the last of the string of plane directors from whom Ev had received guidance instructions. The Spotter, signaling with movements of his arms and hands, motioned for Ev to roll the Phantom forward onto the catapult.

Ev applied an increment of power, rolled up to the bump of the turtle-shell–like shuttle, and then, gingerly applying a little more throttle, eased the wheel of the nose landing gear up and over the shuttle. The plane rocked slightly as the nose landing gear strut moved up and then slid down on the forward side of the shuttle. The jet blast deflector shield rose from the flight deck behind Ev's Phantom, thereby protecting the planes behind from the F-4's hot exhaust blasts. Linfield Two Zero One was surrounded by men wearing various colors. Many hand signals were given and Ev acknowledged each one.

The ground crew then actuated a switch inside the nose landing gear bay that pneumatically extended the nose landing strut to elevate the nose of the Phantom. The nose rose about eighteen inches to put the Phantom in the correct attitude for launch off the catapult and immediate subsequent flight.

Ev was instructed to raise his hands above his head to indicate that he was not touching any controls. Seeing this, ordnance men in red jerseys crawled beneath the plane and removed the arming pins from the Zuni pods and Sparrow missiles. They held them up so that Ev could count them and confirm that his weaponry was now armed and lethal.

Ev and Jack, looking straight down the track of the catapult to the sea beyond, sat alone, ensconced in their aircraft, while people continued working beneath the Phantom in preparation for its launch.

A perfectly milled, high-tensile, steel restraining rod several inches long, called a holdback, or commonly called a "dog bone" or "dumbbell," was inserted into the long shank of a heavy, T-shaped steel restraint. The holdback was then attached to the back of the plane beneath the empennage (tail assembly) in front of the tailhook, beneath and in between the two engines and behind the centerline fuel tank. The holdback, designed to restrain forward movement of the F-4 even in afterburner, would break at a predetermined tension when the catapult was fired. Each plane type had its own restraining rod milled for its specific weight, inertia, thrust, and so on. A restraining rod for an A-4, a lighter aircraft, would not possibly work for an F-4, for example.

Looped ends of a large-diameter steel cable, called a bridle, were placed on large steel hooks that were attached to the plane and positioned astride the fuselage just beneath the leading root of each wing. The middle portion of the bridle was then placed over the shuttle now sitting just behind the nose landing gear. The shuttle was cocked, ready for firing at the back of the catapult. The shuttle-bridle system, once the catapult was fired, would slingshot the F-4 into the sky from the leading edge of the angled deck of *Kitty Hawk*.

In front of and just to one side of the plane, a member of the catapult crew held up a small chalkboard on which was written the gross weight of the plane. Since every plane type, or the load situation for each plane type, is different for every launch, the catapult has to be set for the type of aircraft and its weight and the wind speed over the deck. Ev acknowledged that the gross weight as written was correct and this was shown to the catapult officer to confirm concurrence.

While launches were occurring on the bow catapults and another plane was being positioned on the adjacent waist catapult, the Plane Director signaled to Ev that the Phantom was "going into tension." The shuttle was moved forward to take up the slack in the bridle cable that connected the aircraft to the shuttle. Men wearing white jerseys, the White Shirts, performed one last quality control check to ensure that everything was ready for launch.

The Spotter transferred control of Linfield Two Zero One to the Catapult Officer by pointing both hands directly at him. Ev acknowledged the transfer.

The Catapult Officer continued with the hand signals. He rotated his fingers near his head in a circular motion, known as the "two-finger turn-up." With the pre-launch check complete and this signal given by the Catapult Officer and acknowledged by Ev, Ev pushed the throttles of his F-4 to full military power. The fuel flow gauges jumped, the tachometers registered 100 percent rpm, the nozzle gauges registered the position of the exhaust nozzles that were expelling extremely white-hot gas. The needle of each temperature gauge soared. The compressor and turbine blades of the engines of Linfield Two Zero One whined at a high pitch while hot exhaust gases thundered intolerably out the exhaust ports. The large war plane, restrained by the holdback, shuddered.

The Catapult Officer made a fist and then opened his hand flat, fingers extended. This indicated to Ev to move the throttles forward past the current setting and into afterburner. Ev acknowledged the instruction. He removed his feet from the brakes and, with his left hand, slid the throttles outboard and forward into afterburner position. This caused raw jet fuel to surge directly into the flame at the back of the engine. The noise from the Phantom's exhaust crescendoed even more, like an angry volcano in continuous eruption. Long, intense flames shot out from the exhaust of each engine, the roar of the exhaust now deafening. The super-hot exhaust blast was deflected up by the jet blast deflector. The Phantom, now under the influence of maximum power and thrust, was still restrained from forward movement by the small-diameter steel holdback that connected it to the carrier deck. Each airman prepared himself for the inevitable forward surge of acceleration.

Ev, keeping his eyes on his instruments, braced his head back against the headrest. Without turning his head, and satisfied that Linfield Two Zero One was operating as intended, Ev executed a smart salute which was the signal confirming that the Phantom was ready for launch. Now there was no turning back.

Within the next few seconds, Ev would "rotate off the cat." Correct rotation has to be quick and effective and sufficient to compensate for the load on board and for the airspeed. Too little rotation on the control stick and the plane will sink—and there is only seventy-five feet to the water, not much to play with. Too much rotation and the plane may stall, an equally bad situation. During launch, Ev would be aided by daytime visual peripheral clues that a pilot learns to sense and to which he adjusts.

Ev's right hand held the control stick slightly aft while his left hand secured the throttles in their full forward position. The big Phantom, shaking under the influence of its engines and in anticipation of launch, sat poised.

The A-3 that had launched before Ev off the same catapult had quickly disappeared and was nowhere to be seen. The only thing that could be seen in front of Ev and Jack, beyond the bow of *Kitty Hawk*, was the endless, empty blue sky, the gray-blue of the unforgiving sea; and the faint thin horizontal line in the far distance where the two met.

Outside the cockpit, standing on the flight deck, the Catapult Officer acknowledged Ev's salute and, in one fluid motion, knelt to his right and moved his right arm in an exaggerated arc over his head from left to right and touched two fingers of his right hand to the deck. The flight deck choreography was over. There was no mistaking the signal.

In the catwalk opposite from and in clear view of the Catapult Officer, another man who awaited the launch signal with his hands held high, lowered them and pressed two large side-by-side buttons with his hands. Virtually in the same instant, under the force of both engines in afterburner and under the extreme influence of the sudden acceleration of the catapult, several times greater than that of gravity, the resultant force snapped the perfectly machined steel rod of the holdback restraint. Ev and Jack's F-4, in a loud, ear-splitting roar, trailing hot exhaust, carrying its cargo of deadly Zuni rockets bound for Thanh Hoa, screamed along the short steel runway, two hundred fifty feet to the edge of the angled deck. Each airman, feeling the sudden increase in Gs from the instantaneous acceleration of Linfield Two Zero One, was abruptly pressed back in his seat. Ev, with his right hand firm on the control stick, kept tight forward pressure on the two side-by-side throttles with his left hand, still making sure they remained in their full forward position as the plane accelerated down the short length of the catapult. The world and colors around the two airmen on the deck outside the cockpit blurred as the sea in front of them loomed greater, ready to swallow them. Steam escaped from the open longitudinal slot and blew the length of the catapult track behind the Phantom. Super-hot exhaust gas from the F-4 blasted back toward the catapult crew, its smell piercing the nostrils of each man.

The leading edge of the angled deck of *Kitty Hawk* slid swiftly beneath Linfield Two Zero One. The steel cable bridle that pulled the Phantom down the catapult track and thrust it into the sky, fell from the hooks beneath the plane. Whereas it took several minutes to position and make ready on the catapult a fully loaded aircraft weighing about fifty thousands pounds, the actual launch was completed in about three seconds.

Linfield Two Zero One, with Ev and Jack on board, launched by the unfaltering, awesome force caused by a steam-powered machine, had sailed off the ship from the waist catapult beyond the bow of *Kitty Hawk* over the remorseless blue-gray water. If the sea was hungry for this plane this day, it would have to wait. The F-4, no longer constrained and free from *Kitty Hawk*, was on its own. In the blink of an eye, as its name suggests, the Phantom was gone.

Chapter 17
The Flight of Linfield Two Zero One

THE PHANTOM, SET ON THE CORRECT trajectory off the edge of the angled deck of *Kitty Hawk*, continued to accelerate and, with each passing second, incrementally gained the valuable flying resource known as airspeed.

Now airborne, the flight of Linfield Two Zero One was well underway, Ev reached for the landing gear handle located to the left of the main instrument panel and raised it. The main landing gears retracted into the wings and the nose landing gear rotated up simultaneously into the forward fuselage of the Phantom. The doors closed concealing the landing gears from view. Never knowing with one hundred percent certainty beforehand about the success (or failure) of a launch—but with that now behind them—Ev and Jack and the Phantom that carried them were in a positive climb. The needle of the airspeed indicator continued to point to higher numbers as it rotated incrementally around the dial. Ev pulled back on the throttles and extinguished the afterburner. He reached for the flap control panel and retracted the flaps. Now with less drag, airspeed continued to increase. Linfield Two Zero One, accelerating through 300 knots, continued its robust climb into the blue abyss of the tropical skies over the Gulf of Tonkin. The powerful twin engines sucked in huge quantities of air and expelled equally huge quantities of hot gases. The resultant thrust pushed the F-4 faster, effortlessly. The Phantom was doing exactly what Herman Barkey designed it to do: fly.

The mammoth *Kitty Hawk* was soon left behind and grew smaller, more insignificant, with each passing second as Ev and Jack continued to make their way skyward in their F-4. The plane, encumbered with its load of ordnance and fuel, having lumbered along on the flight deck like a prehistoric behemoth and currently clawing hungrily through the air, was now in its element. The Phantom, seemingly as if it knew its purpose, assuming a life of its own—Ev and Jack unneeded—was on its way to Thanh Hoa.

Back on *Kitty Hawk*, the only remnant now that Ev and Jack's Phantom had ever been positioned on the catapult, or that it had ever existed, was the trail of wafting steam from the catapult groove, the shuttle that was being retracted, now moving aft, and the cutting smell of the Phantom's exhaust that languished briefly.

On the catapult from which Ev and Jack had launched in their Phantom just seconds before, the shuttle was drawn back and repositioned ready for re-activation. The jet blast deflector shield was lowered. The catapult crew and Yellow Shirts immediately turned their attention to make ready the launch of the next aircraft. Other planes were launching in rapid sequence from the other catapults but there were still several planes yet to launch.

During launch, time is a valuable resource not to be squandered; move-ment of aircraft and personnel are precisely coordinated. The launch scenario would be repeated again and again until the entire strike group, made up of individual combat aircraft, was shot from *Kitty Hawk* into the vastness above the Gulf of Tonkin.

The other two Phantoms in Ev and Jack's flight, crewed by Wayne Miller and George Stock; and Phil Brown and Jim Cook, launched behind Ev and Jack. They soon joined up with Linfield Two Zero One. The three F-4s formed up at about 8,000 feet above *Kitty Hawk*.

A-4 and A-6 attack aircraft, with multiple bombs suspended beneath their wings, launched and were climbing to altitude behind the Phantoms.

The last aircraft to launch were an RA-5C Vigilante photo reconnais-sance plane of squadron RVAH-13 piloted by Alexander Wattay with Frank Prendergast as the backseat RAN; and the Vigilante's escort, an F-4B Phan-tom II from VF-213. The RA-5C would take aerial photos of the results of the strike mission.

The entire launch sequence had lasted not more than thirty minutes. *Kitty Hawk* had unleashed the fury of her air wing into the blue skies above the Gulf of Tonkin.

All elements of the strike group soon rendezvoused in the skies above *Kitty Hawk*, joining together into a formidable group of combat aircraft. Each plane within this lethal air formation was designated a specific position and a specific role to be fulfilled during the mission. Once formed up, the strike force headed for the Thanh Hoa Bridge in Route Package IV. The mission to destroy the bridge would not be aborted.

Having identified their location visually, Ev and Jack knew they were southeast of the town of Thanh Hoa. Navigation is performed by the RIO but due to the good visibility that day, Jack did not need any navigational aids. Ev banked their Phantom to a heading of 315 degrees, which would take them and the strike group directly to Thanh Hoa. The two other F-4s followed suit in formation.

The coast and the vague, distant outlines of the Ma River could be seen. Ev and Jack would reach the coastline and the mouth of the river, not more than ninety miles away, in about ten minutes. The target was located about eight miles farther inland.

The strike group from *Kitty Hawk* continued in a northwesterly direction until it was about five miles shy of the coast, at which time the A-4s and A-6s diverted south and the three F-4's headed due north still at an altitude of about 8,000 feet. The Thanh Hoa Bridge was vaguely visible on the horizon to the port side of Linfield Two Zero One.

The three F-4s, now north of their target, proceeded to a point somewhere south of the town of Ninh Binh. Ev and Jack were pleased with how perfect the weather was, how the mission was progressing, and how, so far at that point in the flight when they crossed the shoreline, "feet dry" as the expression goes, everything seemed quiet. The Phantoms had not received any threats to the flight. Nothing menacing was detected.

Jack carried his ship-issued 70mm camera in hopes that he might be able to take some photographs after the strike was completed. He was well known for his photography skills and it had been stated that his pictures were sometimes more useful than those taken by reconnaissance flights. But at this moment, Jack had more urgent business to worry about.

The plan for the F-4 flak suppression mission called for a pop-up to 11,000 feet, the beginning-strike altitude. The three Phantoms increased their altitude from 8,000 feet to 11,000 feet and, in a fluid arcing wing-over maneuver to the left, turned through a westerly heading and then south to a heading of 210 degrees. The flight of three Phantoms prepared for the final run-in to the bridge's air defenses. Ev, with slight, subtle movements of the flight controls and throttles, continued his wing-over arc into a diving attack at the planned, pre-briefed angle of forty-five degrees. The nose of the

F-4 fell through the horizon line. The forward vision from within the cockpit shifted from the white-blue of the sky to the brown-green of the earth.

Ev had armed the Zuni rockets by throwing a toggle switch on the console that sat to his right and a little below the instruments that he scanned continuously. Ev and the two other F-4 pilots would fire their Zuni rockets at 5,000 feet, followed by the planes' pullout at no lower than 3,000 feet. Once the attack was initiated, at around 500 miles per hour, this altitude difference would be covered very quickly.

After having released the Zunis, the F-4s were to return to *Kitty Hawk* cruising a predetermined course, still on its foxtrot corpen, in the Gulf of Tonkin somewhere southeast of Thanh Hoa. If flying at night or under instrument flight conditions, the F-4s would have returned first to a predetermined area referred to as "marshal," for eventual recovery one plane at a time, on board *Kitty Hawk*, the same carrier from which they had been launched. But for daytime missions similar to this one, returning aircraft normally returned overhead and circled until the next launch was complete; then they would descend for recovery.

Now flying south and in a steep, attacking dive, Ev and Jack scanned their instruments. The Phantom was operating perfectly. Jack called out altitude and airspeed—9,000 feet, 400 knots; 8,500 feet, 420 knots; 8,000 feet, 440 knots—from the back seat of Linfield Two Zero One. All engine instruments on Linfield Two Zero One registered that the engines were operating within normal parameters. Ev pressed his diving attack.

As Linfield Two Zero One neared the Thanh Hoa Bridge from the north, sharp, pointed staccato flashes could be seen on the ground. The sky began to fill quickly with instant puffs of smoke from exploding invisible projectiles that were fired from antiaircraft artillery. They exploded loudly and violently. The flak barrage increased. Soon the sky became thick with black and white cloudlets of smoke. The flight had been detected by the defenders who had surmised this strike was not a deception: Without question the primary target was again their beloved Ham Rong Bridge.

The flak became thicker. Each explosive burst rocked the plane. Though buffeted around from the nearby explosions, Ev maintained control of Linfield Two Zero One's onward, downward progress with the other two F-4s in the flight immediately following a little behind and spread to either side.

Although visible through the front of the canopy, Ev did not notice the silhouette of the Thanh Hoa Bridge or the blackened steel members of the bridge trusses that had been damaged from previous attacks. His focus was the air defenses of the bridge not the bridge itself. The air defenses, the flak sites—olive green antiaircraft (triple-A) guns within earthen embankments— and other emplacements were within clear sight. His targets were in the flat tidal area immediately to the right of the bridge and also the gun emplacements on the small hillock (Nui Ngoc) just to the left of the bridge.

Roaring downward through the blanket of flak toward their targets, Ev and Jack were about to destroy the same guns that were firing at them. Miller and Stock and Brown and Cook followed Ev and Jack. They would attack the guns on either side of Linfield Two Zero One's targets.

Ev continued the F-4's steep descent to 5,000 feet. True to the plan of attack, at this precise altitude Ev depressed the firing button on the control stick and the Zuni rockets, one by one but in very rapid succession, ignited and fired toward their targets from the rocket pods. The other F-4s fired their load of Zuni rockets too. Soon the sky was filled not only with bursts from antiaircraft shells and tracer rounds from ZPUs, but with thick exhaust trails from dozens of Zuni rockets. The effect was like a salvo.

The Zuni rockets screamed toward their targets at speeds much faster than the Phantoms were flying. Ev could only surmise the explosions of the warheads and the resulting destruction and the havoc the Zunis would create on the ground as they struck the antiaircraft emplacements. The warheads of each rocket ignited just above the ground, scattering deadly shrapnel over a wide area. The noise would be deafening. Little could survive such an onslaught of air-to-surface weaponry.

With all Zuni rockets released, it was now time for the Phantoms to egress the area and let the A-4s and A-6s complete the job of destroying the bridge. Ev and Jack had succeeded in their mission. Surely the strike by the Phantoms had compromised some, hopefully most, of the air defenses of the Thanh Hoa Bridge. They had accomplished what they had been sent from *Kitty Hawk*, sailing in the Gulf of Tonkin, or in a more esoteric sense, all the way from San Diego, to Thanh Hoa to do. They could now disappear over the horizon and return to the safety of *Kitty Hawk*.

But things were not right with Linfield Two Zero One. Immediately after firing the Zunis, something went wrong with Ev and Jack's Phantom. After

Ev first fired the Zunis at 5,000 feet and just before he was to pull back on the control stick and ease the two throttles forward, he felt a sharp thud from somewhere in the fuselage. Jack heard a loud bang in the starboard engine and, having previously moved his head to the right so he could see past Ev, he was startled to see flames shoot out the front of the starboard air intake. Ev, intent on the mission, did not see the flames but with his ears attuned to the engines and his eyes alert to the information displayed on the instruments before him, knew immediately that he had a malfunction in the starboard engine. The symptoms could be likened to compressor stall or compressor stagnation. But in a technical sense neither occurred. A large piece of shrapnel and possibly debris from the Zuni rockets had slammed into the starboard engine and sheered off at least three stator vanes forcing them back into the compressor blades, causing considerable damage to the first several stages of the compressor.

"*Jack, we've flamed out!*" Ev stated loudly; or so Ev thought for a moment.

His quick glance at the right exhaust gas temperature gauge, however, indicated otherwise. The temperature in the starboard engine was beginning to rise inordinately. Ev scrutinized the right column of engine instruments in an attempt to ascertain what may be wrong with the starboard engine. He noted that while there was continued fuel flow, there was a sudden loss of rpm.

The danger of this mission was behind them; San Diego was not far away—at least, that is what Ev and Jack would have preferred to think. Had the situation been different for Ev and Jack, the flight back to *Kitty Hawk* would have been easy, even uneventful, and would have taken less than twenty minutes. The weather was clear. But the mighty, indomitable F-4 was crippled. Ev's mind and professional skill turned to reversing this unfavorable circumstance. Although *Kitty Hawk* was not far away, at the moment, Ev had many pressing problems to manage before he could reach the safety of the ship.

The situation deteriorated further. Ev's eyes scanned the left column of engine instruments; the information being displayed for the port engine was chilling. The port engine was not operating normally either! The tachometer and temperature gauges for the port engine registered a sudden loss of rpm and a rapid increase in temperature, similar to what the instruments for the starboard engine were displaying. At almost precisely the same moment as the starboard engine began to malfunction, the turbine section of the port engine had been hit by shrapnel. The turbine blades were severely damaged, to the point that rotation of the blades was greatly reduced.

With neither engine performing at full rpm or providing full thrust, the electrical generators would fail to produce sufficient electrical power; the plane would lose its electrical systems. And with the temperature rising in both engines, with a fuel tank located immediately above them, the aircraft could explode.

Roaring through the air, continuing on the same heading, with flak from the undamaged guns following them, Ev and Jack's crippled Phantom flew over the north, or east end of the bridge and crossed the Ma River northeast of Thanh Hoa City. Ev recovered from the dive, his field of vision immediately shifting from the green, muddy brown of the ground to the horizon and the much brighter blue of the sky. Now over the flats on the south side of the Ma River, Ev slowly turned the Phantom in a long arc to the left, the HSI now rotating off 210 degrees toward 200 degrees; the horizon line in his ADI rose to mimic the attitude of the plane.

Both airmen knew they were in danger.

Jack, not having visual access to the engine instruments from the back seat, could only surmise the gravity of the situation. But he didn't need instruments to tell him what was obvious: neither engine in their F-4 was working to its full capacity. Linfield Two Zero One had been damaged. Their Phantom was seriously injured. Because they were low, unless the situation changed very quickly and favorably, it would become grim.

Ev became very busy in the front seat. He furthered his shallow arc to the left over and just east of Thanh Hoa City toward the sea, turning the plane south. As the left wing dipped slightly to his left, the HSI, its compass face rotating in the opposite direction of the turn, registered the Phantom's changing heading briefly to 190 degrees, then 180 degrees, 170 degrees, 160, 150.

The Phantom more or less paralleled the Ma River. Jack could see the muddy water and the small huts and buildings along the river's bank off the lowered left wingtip. Ahead, through the opaque atmosphere, the mouth of the river was faintly visible. Jack could hear the engines turning but he knew that at least one was heavily damaged and he surmised the other may have flamed out.

For a jet fighter aircraft (or any plane for that matter), flight controls and the flight itself are dependent on airspeed. Without benefit of engines, speed means descending, and descending means losing valuable altitude. Linfield Two Zero One was losing altitude as Ev traded altitude for flying speed. The Phantom's engines continued to lose rpm, which fell below generator-operating speed. Electrical power was gone.

Without an intercom, it was necessary for Jack to remove his oxygen mask so he could communicate with Ev. Jack yelled, *"Put the RAT out!"* and then repositioned his oxygen mask.

Ev reached back just behind his left shoulder and pulled a small yellow T-lever with the letters "R-A-T" written on it.

The ram air turbine (RAT), not really a turbine at all, consists of a small propeller (about fourteen inches in diameter) of twin opposing blades that, like an electric windmill, drives a small electrical generator. The entire system is attached at the end of a short, sturdy steel arm which reclines and is hidden in a small bay on the upper left side of the fuselage, about mid-fuselage, behind the airmen. The RAT is concealed by two opposing clamshell-like doors that open and allow the arm with the rotor head to rotate upward out of its hidden position. Activated by pulling the yellow T-handle, pneumatic pressure caused the clamshell-like doors to spring open and the RAT immediately to rotate out of its concealed bay. Once exposed to the air stream, the twin propellers would drive a generator and restore or augment essential electrical power.

Now, below 3,000 feet, certainly not much altitude, Jack, surmising he and Ev may have to eject, said, *"Let's get to the river."*

Ev trimmed the Phantom to its optimum glide slope by manipulating the trim button on the top of the control stick. The optimal glide slope would allow for enough airflow over the control surfaces of the wings for them to respond to commands from the pilot. But airflow meant airspeed and without sufficient thrust from the engines this meant a nose-down attitude. Ev maintained a slight downward slope so that altitude would not be sacrificed too quickly. Phantoms are not long on gliding. To reach beyond the coast to the safety of the sea, where he and Jack could eject and be rescued by helicopter, Ev needed about 15,000 to 20,000 feet of altitude, a valuable resource he did not have.

Still, more or less on a southerly heading, Ev maintained the plane at its optimum glide slope and turned his attention to the engines. He did not know the extent of the damage to either engine but knew that neither one could provide the thrust needed. It was unlikely that he could correct the situation now existing with each engine. More seriously, each engine was overheating due to uncontrolled flames, but at this point at least the flames were contained within the engines.

Ev scanned the parallel vertical rows of engine instruments on the right panel. He saw that the rpm for both engines were very low and faltering. The engine compressors and turbines, connected by the same shaft, were turning, that much he knew.

But while there were reduced rpm and decreased thrust, of more serious consequence, the needles of the temperature gauges kept indicating higher than normal maximum operating temperature, which is usually about six hundred forty degrees centigrade. Ev saw the needle for each gauge point at or a little above the number "8" on the dial. This meant the engines were registering a little more than eight hundred degrees Centigrade (1,472 Fahrenheit), a very unpleasant situation indeed.

Knowing he was stricken and too low and too slow to cover the eight or so miles to the coast, Ev had one objective that was aligned with Jack's comment: he was going to try to make it to the Ma River and the safety of water. The Ma River would be Ev and Jack's only chance of survival. If he could just make it to the river, the two airmen would be at less risk of capture after their ejection. They would have a better chance of eluding their captors. There would be a good possibility that U.S. Navy rescue helicopters could extract them from the muddy river and away from the clutches of the North Vietnamese.

Ev continued angling more easterly toward the widest part of the Ma River. His HSI rotated down in numbers through 140 degrees. With the trim button on the top of his control stick, he continued adjusting the plane's flight to its optimum glide slope in an attempt to maintain flying airspeed and to gain as much distance as he could—a tradeoff between rate of sink and distance. But starting from around 5,000 feet at the Thanh Hoa Bridge, Ev didn't have much room to maneuver.

Ev was losing altitude quickly. He maintained airspeed but with neither engine producing full thrust, all he could do was continue to adjust the Phantom's attitude to keep the plane flying. The situation facing the two American airmen from *Kitty Hawk*, just days before their return to San Diego, was not promising. Ev knew he was inevitably destined to run out of altitude, and very soon. Ejection from the stricken Phantom was imminent.

Linfield Two Zero One, with its two occupants on board, arced through the skies of Route Package IV deep in enemy territory. Like a chariot driver who tries to lead his injured horses and damaged chariot out of harm's way after a battle, Ev was guiding his wounded Phantom away from the enemy. The Phantom tried to respond, to obey Ev's commands as best it could, but airspeed as well as all of the F-4's systems were dependent on the life-giving engines that were now failing.

The Flight of Linfield Two Zero One which had begun so robustly was about to end. Ev knew the Phantom was lost. If Ev could have saved the Phantom, he would have. He now had to focus only on saving his and Jack's lives. Ev turned the Phantom a little more east, the HSI rotated through 130 degrees, finally settling on a heading of 120 degrees. Ev paid no attention to the HSI. He aimed for a wide spot in the Song Ma, where the river straightens out towards the sea—it was the best he could do. The river was his last and only option. And then, his luck ran out.

Jack, witnessing the events as best he could from the back seat, prepared himself for the ominous prospect of ejection. He was, for all intents and purposes, along for the ride—at this point an observer. This was not going to be good. He placed his 70mm camera on the floor of his cockpit between his feet in preparation for the inevitable.

The flight manual for the F-4 contains charts that provide minimum parameters for ejection at various speeds and flight attitudes. But Ev didn't need any chart to explain the situation that confronted him. So low were he and Jack, without the possibility of gaining more altitude or increasing their airspeed, and now with the tops of fifty-foot-high trees passing quickly by on both sides, just shy of the Ma River, Ev knew he had no options left. They wouldn't make the river. The Phantom was going to crash. If they didn't escape now, they would die. Depressing the intercom button on his microphone, Ev issued his last instruction as flight leader and aircraft commander of the Phantom that was Linfield Two Zero One. *"Jack, get out! Get out now!"*

Jack immediately pulled the ejection seat firing handle down from over his head to activate his ejection seat. The face curtain that would be drawn down would protect his face from the blast of onrushing air. But Jack changed his mind. He wanted to see what was happening and released the handle before it had an opportunity to ignite the explosive charges that would propel the ejection seat upward.

Jack made his last transmission over the radio from Linfield Two Zero One: "*Tell my wife I won't be home for dinner.*"

Using a second ejection option, Jack pulled up quickly on the handle found between his knees. The rear canopy exploded away and, with the three progressive charges exploding in the tube behind his back, Jack, strapped into his ejection seat with his legs automatically pulled in tautly, was ejected within a quarter second of activation out the top of the F-4 from the back seat of the plane.

Immediately after Jack's ejection, there was a second explosion and Ev's canopy, in front of where Jack had been, was blown away. Ev's seat, with him strapped firmly into it, also suddenly left the plane.

Bereft of its crew and suddenly lighter by about six hundred pounds, the now crewless Phantom, with no pilot to give it commands—as if it mattered at this point—thundered along for not more than another three, maybe four seconds before crashing into the tidal flats of the Ma River at the northwesterly tip of a flat, narrow, treeless island. The Phantom belly-smashed into the mud, snapping off its plastic radome (enclosure for the radar) and the forward part of the fuselage just in front of the cockpit. In addition to burying its nose, the aircraft landed with one wing low and spun around in the mud, coming to rest pointing northwest.

The Navy F-4B Phantom II, the creation of Herman Barkey in St. Louis, bearing the numbers *201* and *3001* on each side of its fuselage, launched from the deck of the USS *Kitty Hawk*, lay in the dark mud of the Ma River. The flight of Linfield Two Zero One was over. The Phantom would never fly again.

Chapter 18
Search and Rescue (but not quite) for Ev and Jack

THE CREWS OF THE OTHER PHANTOMS in Ev and Jack's flight knew that Linfield Two Zero One was down. Word was relayed from the Phantom crews back to *Kitty Hawk* that Linfield Two Zero One was spotted in the Ma River virtually intact, but the whereabouts of the two airmen could not be ascertained. Soon, A-6s from the bombing strike patrolled overhead trying to see if they could find either airman. They could not. One A-6 crew from VA-85 circled above Linfield Two Zero One for thirty minutes and relayed coordinates and additional information about the downed F-4 to *Kitty Hawk*.

Due to the acute level of American combat air activity in Vietnam, the United States deployed a cruiser off the shores of North Vietnam and aircraft in the skies over South Vietnam to monitor all air frequencies and direct attacks or rescue missions, and to advise American aviators on issues that would have a direct bearing on them or their rescue.

Through coordinated search and rescue (SAR) efforts, the collective SAR-related aircraft monitored missions throughout the area and provided airborne guidance based on information from powerful radars and communication equipment on board the aircraft. They were instrumental in saving the lives of many downed American airmen and their role became integral to the overall air campaign.

SAR was a comfort to airmen as they flew into combat because they knew that someone would be on their side. SAR would be their last hope for a safe rescue. Search and rescue efforts succeeded many times, but were not always successful with every incident. In the case of Linfield Two Zero One, such was the case.

On 14 May 1967, SAR-related aircraft were busy as usual monitoring many attack missions into North Vietnam by the Air Force as well as by the

Navy and other air activities in South Vietnam. At around 16:00 hours (4:00 p.m.) Vietnam time, they received information, probably from one or both of the other F-4s that flew on Ev and Jack's wing, about a downed Phantom that was now resting in a river not far from Thanh Hoa. The airmen noted the coordinates of Linfield Two Zero One thus providing the initial basis for the search and rescue effort.

SAR initiated action. The ensuing transcribed dialogue involving coded elements of the search and rescue are sketchy but give a glimpse of the overall picture as to what transpired after Ev and Jack ejected. The dialogue between various obscure, coded entities or call signs begins at 8:05 Zulu (Greenwich Mean Time), or 4:05 p.m. Vietnam time and ends thirty-nine minutes later at 8:44 Zulu, or 4:44 p.m. Vietnam time.

Crown 5 (an airborne C-130): *Linfield Two Zero One has punched out at one niner, four six north: one zero five, five zero east. Crown B proceeding.*

Queen: *I advise Crown Five and B to remain twenty nautical miles offshore.*

Queen: *Crown Five, request Arabs* [Navy A-1s] *into the area. Be advised Warpaint* [A-4Es] *in area as is Linfield Two Zero Six. Two S-O-Bs* [souls on board].

Crown 5: *Clementine 02* [Navy rescue helicopter] *has launched.*

Crown 5: *A-4s on station and will be going into area.*

Queen: *Crown Five and B, now advise: remain thirty nautical miles offshore.*

Compress (U.S. Air Force SAR Control): *Crown Two, request relay. Jolly Green Zero Nine and Five Two* [two USAF HH-3s] *on cockpit alert.*

Crown 5: *Two chutes spotted. Negative Beeper yet. Linfield 201 wreckage spotted in water. Coordinates good.*

Crown 5: *No contact with Linfield 201. Aircraft is in water and will be destroyed.*

Crown 5: *Negative beeper on Linfield.*

The U.S. Navy, exhausting its efforts and with daylight passing to dusk, transmits one last message:

Be advised, SAR on Linfield Alpha Charlie suspended at 10:20 Zulu (6:20p.m. Vietnam time).

The time is important to note because night falls in the tropics like a curtain at about 7:00 p.m. No further search and rescue communication was recorded.

Chapter 19
After the Action

AIRCREWS REALLY DID NOT CARE TO FILL out the five or six, long pages of after-action reports upon returning to their aircraft carriers from an air combat mission. To some it may have seemed meaningless or an annoying inconvenience, to others simply a tedious task to be avoided. These were seldom signed so there was no way of knowing who filled out the forms.

The after-action reports for the various strikes on the Thanh Hoa Bridge on 14 May 1967 consistently indicated unlimited ceiling, clear weather or, as some stated, scattered clouds at about 4,000 feet and a few at 1,200 feet. Visibility was at ten nautical miles or, as stated in some reports, unobstructed. The terrain was flat or rolling. Consistent with the other reports, the after-action report for Ev and Jack's flight of three Phantoms, the information for which would have been provided by Miller and Stock, and Brown and Cook, indicated flat terrain, a ceiling of about 1,500 feet, broken cloud cover and no obstruction to visibility. In summation, excepting some cloud cover, the weather and visibility that day were good.

The after-action reports for the flight of three F-4s confirmed they carried Zuni rockets for the flak suppression mission. Further, the reports indicated they were effective at suppressing the air defenses surrounding the Thanh Hoa Bridge just prior to the main the strike.

It is the other information, however, that is of more interest.

The after-action reports described the antiaircraft defenses in the vicinity of the Thanh Hoa Bridge. The reports indicated a large quantity and wide dispersal of 37mm antiaircraft artillery. The pilots noted many solitary gun positions and in one report several emplacements with four to six 37mm guns contained in each. Other calibers of air defense flak units, namely 12.7mm, 14.5mm machine guns and 57mm and 85mm antiaircraft guns were noted too. The 37mm antiaircraft gun seemed to be the most prolific. No sighting of SAMs was reported.

The reports suggested medium and, at one point, heavy flak with gray and black bursts at an altitude of 5,000 to 7,000 feet. Pilots registered and noted on their reports barrage fire from 12.7mm and 14.5mm antiaircraft units. Other reports for strikes that followed the initial strike indicated light flak.

The bomb damage assessment (BDA) reports for the strike actions on 14 May provided by the attack squadrons (those squadrons that made the actual bomb runs), indicated that the bridge sustained hits and was damaged but did not fall. One A-4 pilot from VA-112 observed, "*The bridge received good hits but is still up.*" Another A-4 pilot from the same squadron reported, "*Good hits, no BDA due to smoke.*" Another VA-112 report stated, "*Put good hits on western abutment to the bridge. No BDA due to smoke.*" Yet another pilot, still from VA-112 reported, "*Montana struck the bridge. Target tracking very difficult due to smoke. No BDA due to smoke. Very little AAA encountered on the target.*"

Alexander Wattay and Frank Prendergast, flying in their RA-5C Vigilante with their F-4 escort from VF-213, arrived over the Thanh Hoa Bridge only moments after the strike. They were the last planes of the mission. After the photo-surveillance run, the two planes departed the environs of Thanh Hoa unscathed and returned safely to *Kitty Hawk.*

Wattay noted in his after-action report: "*Photo pilot flew over Thanh Hoa Bridge and reports bridge still standing. Unable to determine if damaged.*" Al Wattay's photographs, capturing the image of black, broiling clouds of thick smoke billowing high above the bridge, showed the awesome destructive power of the strike.

But that was not all the reports revealed.

Miller and Stock, and Brown and Cook, noted in a report appended to their after-action report that details aircraft loss/damage/abortion/diversion, the "Combat Loss" of Linfield 201—(BuNo) 153001 in RP-IV at 08:00 Zulu at coordinates 19-46-40N,105-50-08E.

A/C [aircraft] evidently flamed out. Pilot called both engines had quit. Both pilot and RIO ejected—Two good chutes. No beepers heard. Unknown if A/C was damaged by Air Defenses.

Crew Status:

544716 LCDR Southwick: M.

633926 LT Rollins: M.

They also noted at the bottom of the first page for Mission Data: "Lin 201—Believe to have expended ordnance on AAA site."

The report from an A-6 crew from VA-85 that circled over the downed Phantom stated, "*Saw A/C in the river. Orbited area for half hour. Received no beeper signals.*"

Recognizing from radio reports that an intact F-4 was seen in the Ma River and would soon be analyzed by the North Vietnamese and probably the Russians, the U.S. Navy either diverted some aircraft from their primary mission or launched new aircraft to target and destroy the downed American fighter jet. The after-action reports for those aircraft indicated the effort expended to destroy Ev and Jack's Phantom. A-4 pilots from VA-112 noted, "Hit downed F-4B from VF-114 and put bombs on it." A-4 pilots from VA-144, and another A-4 from VA-112 had multiple missions late on 14 May. The primary target, however, became the destruction of Linfield Two Zero One. The report noted, "*The flight of 4 A/C [aircraft] diverted to destroy a downed aircraft. The A/C was in the Song Ma River and only an oil slick was visible.*" More specifically, the report yields, "*Target A: Downed F-4 A/C; all ordnance on target, probably destroyed A/C.*" The ordnance they dropped were sixteen Mk82 (500-pound) bombs and eight Mk81 (250-pound) bombs.

Sometime, perhaps a day or so later, Alexander Wattay, in his RA-5C, returned to the Thanh Hoa area to photograph Linfield Two Zero One and flew over the site of the downed Phantom from VF-114. Wattay took photographs showing the Phantom in the mud flats of the Song Ma surrounded by bomb craters. In contrast to some of the previous after-action reports, the aircraft appeared undamaged. His was the last aerial photograph of the Phantom in the river, the last visible record of Linfield Two Zero One before it was moved and concealed by the North Vietnamese.

Chapter 20
Laughter throughout the Night: Search for the *Con Ma*

SVEN OSTE, A SWEDISH JOURNALIST WORKING for *Dagens Nyheter* (*Daily News*), Sweden's large daily newspaper published in Stockholm, happened to be near Thanh Hoa on 14 May 1967.

Oste had heard about the air strike on the Thanh Hoa Bridge and the downing of one, possibly two, American fighter bombers. He heard a rumor that one of the planes had landed in one piece, intact, and that the Americans had attempted to destroy it by bombing it. Word from the province commander was that the American plane, a *Con ma*, was near the coast in, or close to, the mouth of the Song Ma. "*We wanted to see the wreck*," Oste reported. He requested permission to search for the plane, to make a report on it.

Oste received permission from the province commander at around 9:00 p.m to try to find the plane and set out by jeep in search of the wreckage. He heard voices all about and realized many people evidently knew of the American plane. They were out searching for it just like he was. A few hours later, Oste encountered clusters of flickering lanterns and smaller lights as groups of people of all ages searched for the wreckage. He later commented that he saw small lights blinking through the darkness over the tidal flats. The wind was redolent of salt from the sea as he and others stumbled along the dark foot paths. He felt certain he was getting nearer the spot where the fighter jet had landed. Oste observed that farmers, teenagers, and the local militia seemed in an excited mood while they searched. There was an energized air of exhilaration. The local inhabitants wanted to find and see up close the wreckage of the American plane so as to confirm or provide proof of a grand victory over a fallen American air monster.

But Oste wanted to ascertain something more. He wanted to try to answer what he thought was a continuing conundrum: the question as to which side was lying the most about American plane losses. In his mind, North Vietnam seemed to exaggerate the losses while the U.S. seemed to understate them.

Oste eventually encountered some men who knew where the plane was. The tide had come in. To see the plane, he would have to enlist the help of a local villager to take him by a small fishing boat to its location. The boatman inched the boat forward slowly, feeling in the water beneath him with his arms for any unexploded bomb. The journey took about two hours but eventually Oste saw a concentration of small flashlights of the searchers and felt he was now very near the plane. Then, suddenly before him, there it was: an American fighter bomber, half submerged in the tidal water. Oste identified it as an F-4B Phantom II and made note of the number on its side—"3001"—and what would turn out to be the squadron: VF-114. Without realizing it, of course, he was looking at Linfield Two Zero One, the Phantom flown by Ev and Jack. Even though the U.S. Navy tried to bomb it and pilots from VA-112 reported it damaged, the F-4 in fact appeared unscathed.

Local citizens were busy placing brush and tree limbs on the plane to camouflage it. Oste observed that the place was crawling with people and everyone was in a carnival mood. They laughed in the dark as if at some party. The carcass of the sinister *may bay my*, the American air giant, lay helpless in the mud.

Oste observed that the airmen obviously tried to make for open water so as to facilitate a helicopter rescue. In talking with the crowds, Oste learned from one man that had the American pilots kept the plane in the air another few seconds they would probably have been rescued. "*Therefore they had waited until the last second to eject…*" and, not having made the river, landed "*…with their parachutes in several mud puddles not far from their plane.*"

Oste had heard that the two airmen had been rounded up, stripped of their flight suits and gear, and beaten before being carted off. While making his way to the landing spot, Oste met some farmers. With a surge of venomous words and gestures and sadistic bursts of laughter, the farmers told Oste about the events that occurred when the two pilots were captured.

Oste never did find the supposed second American fighter jet rumored to have fallen, and he never saw the aircrew of Linfield Two Zero One. In fact, after that night, no one in Thanh Hoa ever saw the two airmen again.

The next day U.S. authorities in Saigon confirmed that there had been a raid on the Thanh Hoa Bridge the day before and, without divulging its location, that the Navy had lost an F-4B aircraft during the strike. There was no comment about the loss of a second aircraft.

Although Oste thought this incident would present a good chance to discover who was lying most about U.S. aircraft losses, he never found an answer.

Sven Oste published his account in *Dagens Nyheter* on 29 May 1967.

Chapter 21
Captured!

BOTH AIRMEN, IMMEDIATELY AFTER THEIR EJECTION, were now free from their F-4. They were reduced to projectiles in space but were relatively safe from imminent death. The situation would devolve, however, the men's safety soon in question. Gravity became the prevailing influence and as it acted on each airman, the circumstances under which they landed were very different.

With a sudden loud explosion in the rear cockpit, Jack had been ejected from the stricken Phantom. The plane fell away from him as the ejection seat rose in the air, the intricate details of his cockpit immediately fading downward and away. Just as Jack had pulled the ejection handle located between his knees, he saw that the camera he had placed between his feet was still on the floor of the back cockpit, but it now fell away from him too with the Phantom.

The operational sequence of the Martin-Baker ejection seat had been activated. After Jack left the plane, still in his seat, the drogue-chute gun located to the left of Jack just behind his shoulder, exploded and sent the heavy projectile out of its tube to pull out the drogue chute. But Jack's face curtain, which he had activated by pulling down first on the overhead ejection handle and had subsequently released, may have interfered with the designed deployment of the drogue chute. Or perhaps it was possible that during some maintenance on board *Kitty Hawk*, the ejection seat may not have been properly installed or its mechanisms not hooked up correctly. There is no way to know. In any event, full completion of the ejection cycle had been fouled. Neither the drogue chute nor the main chute could open. Without benefit of the stabilizing effects of the drogue chute, Jack and his seat tumbled forward. The Phantom had disappeared. As Jack completed a partial rotation forward, the ground passed beneath him and he found himself hurtling through the air on his back, feet first. That was the last thing he saw on the flight of Linfield Two Zero One. The straps and pins that secured him in his seat released automatically and Jack was freed from his ejection seat. The last thing remaining in the ejection sequence was for the main parachute to blossom into what is called a good chute. But Jack's ejection process never reached that point.

Without a fully deployed parachute to slow his forward movement and his descent, the laws of physics were not in Jack's favor. He had been propelled upward but his body was still flying horizontally through space at about the same speed as the Phantom. With the forward, almost horizontal velocity combined with the now downward vertical speed of his body as it accelerated due to gravitational forces, the resulting vector plunged Jack earthward at an oblique angle to the ground. His body slammed into the mud of a rice paddy. He hit the rice paddy still horizontal, feet first. Jack's ejection seat crashed into the mud not far from him at the same moment. Although not rendered unconscious, the air was knocked out of Jack's lungs. The combination of the slanting angle of impact and the deep, thick, black mud had broken his fall.

Now, lying in the mud and still wearing his helmet and oxygen mask, Jack was submerged beneath about one foot of water, which had immediately closed over his oxygen mask and face. Jack kicked himself up and out of the mud. He tried to remove his oxygen mask. Due to his injury, his fingers were numb. He could not release the clips that secured the mask to his helmet with his fingers. He reached behind his head and, with his fists, nudged his helmet forward off his head. At about that time, an A-4 flew overhead in a dive; Jack thought this was not the best place to be because he figured the plane was going to bomb the area.

Jack did not know it yet but his back and hip were broken in several places. A little luckier perhaps, he was to discover later that neither his legs nor arms had been broken. Although injured, he had survived the ejection and the impact of his body with earth. Jack, with his helmet now off, was somehow able to remove his radio from his survival vest to try to contact one of the planes in the flight. He didn't make contact.

Ev was more fortunate than his RIO. His ejection process had worked as intended. Ev had pulled down on the looped lever located above his head and pulled the face curtain over his helmet and visor. The canopy was immediately blown off and then the ejection seat fired, sending it skyward. Immediately out of the cockpit, the drogue-chute gun fired behind Ev's left shoulder, sending the heavy projectile into the sky and causing the drogue chute itself to deploy. The drogue chute blossomed and pulled out the main chute, which deployed into a full canopy, a "good chute," as the expression goes. The harness was released. Ev was pulled from the ejection seat but, at such a low altitude, he didn't even swing through one arc before he hit the ground about three hundred feet from the river and, as he would later learn, several hundred feet from where Jack had landed in a rice paddy.

Ev, landing on the opposite side of the levee from Jack, landed on his feet at the edge of a banana grove not even a second after his parachute had fully blossomed. He did not have time to prepare for the abrupt descent and landing; and the momentum caused him immediately to fall on his back. The parachute fell on him and covered him. It was Ev's second ejection from a stricken F-4 within the last several weeks.

Both men were alive.

Neither airman saw the other as he ejected, and neither witnessed the fate of the Phantom. Ev and Jack, flying from *Kitty Hawk* through the skies of Route Package IV over Thanh Hoa only moments before, had descended onto the soil of North Vietnam along the banks of the Ma River and immediately thereafter into the hands of the North Vietnamese – captives.

Within seconds, villagers surrounded Jack, cursing, yelling and screaming. They didn't try to stand him up. They cut at his G-suit and flight suit and tore them from his body. They cut his boot laces and ripped his boots from his feet, and then they forced Jack's hands behind his back. But just before they bound and cinched up his hands behind him, someone ran up to Jack, ripped his Rolex watch from his wrist, and then scurried away.

Jack was unable to stand. The Vietnamese could not lift such a large man and they let him lie in the mud while a rope was placed around his neck. Now with his hands tied behind his back, and the rope cinched up tightly, Jack was dragged some distance away through the mud to the levee. As Jack's captors pulled him to the top of the levee, they realized that Jack was choking. They loosened the rope from around his neck and pulled him to his feet. The rope had burned his neck.

Jack saw some movement out of the corner of his eye. A man leaped forward with a homemade knife with a blade that resembled a hacksaw blade. Jack tried to dodge the knife attack but was unsuccessful. The attacker stabbed Jack in the right shoulder and left the knife embedded in his flesh. As Jack was being stabbed, a group of men in uniform, evidently of some local militia force, arrived and gained control of the situation. They saved Jack from being killed by his North Vietnamese captors.

Jack's back and lower extremities were without feeling and he had little use of his arms or hands, numb and trussed up as they were. Jack was also in pain from the stab wound in his shoulder. Covered in mud and with blood oozing from his shoulder wound, Jack, barely able to walk, was led to a hut several hundred feet away in which he was placed. Soon a medical person arrived, removed the knife from Jack's shoulder and cleaned and dressed the wound. Jack did not see Ev and had no idea about his status.

Some distance away, although not injured by his ejection, Ev's treatment at the hands of his captors was no better. The chute material had collapsed and fallen on top of him, covering his entire body. Ev pulled the material from over his head only to find he was face to face with the muzzle of an old single-shot rifle that a villager was aiming directly at his face. Ev thought he was going to be shot. The old man motioned for Ev to move. Unlike Jack, Ev could walk easily and was led at gun point to the levee and forced to climb its earthen embankment. Once on the levee, the villagers surrounded and attacked him viciously. They tore and cut at his clothes; everything was taken from him. At one point, he felt something, perhaps a rock, stab or hit him hard in his back.

Ev heard planes flying above. Perhaps they were searching for him and Jack, and a rescue attempt would soon follow. He heard rumbling explosions from the area of the Thanh Hoa Bridge and knew that combat action was still in progress.

The large crowd of angry villagers surrounding Ev pressed in on him. Each wanted a piece of the action as they closed their ranks around him. Even with U.S. aircraft still in the area, villagers raced from their homes to join the melee on the banks of the Song Ma.

"*Come with me*," Ev heard a man say in perfect English. Ev was to realize later that had it not been for this middle-aged, good looking Eurasian man, he may have been killed.

Ev was tied up and taken to a small hut near the levee and placed inside. He had no indications about Jack's fate.

With the militia present, the villagers were less prone to violence. After sundown, a jeep-like vehicle arrived to take the two airmen away. When

Jack was placed into the back of the jeep, he realized he was with Ev. Ev was relieved to know Jack had survived. Both men were still securely tied and blindfolded. Ev's blindfold was secure but not tight. Although his vision was obscured, he was still able to see what was going on around him. Jack's blindfold was made out of some sort of netting material and he could still partially see.

The jeep kept stalling. Eventually the two airmen were transferred into the back of a military truck with a canvas top open at the back. Ev and Jack were driven along the levee toward Thanh Hoa to a small village where the vehicle veered south away from the river to a wider paved thoroughfare, and then north again. Soon they were in Thanh Hoa.

Leaving Thanh Hoa hours after dark, Ev and Jack were transported north toward Hanoi. They crossed the Song Ma and passed the ruins of the air defenses they had attacked and destroyed that afternoon. The vehicle stopped many times to allow convoys headed south to pass. Somewhere between Ninh Binh and Phu Ly, before morning, the truck arrived at what seemed a small camouflaged military staging area or encampment. Ev and Jack were placed in a room of some small building. They were given some tea and water but nothing to eat.

A short time later, local inhabitants or villagers were allowed to enter and pass through the room to see the American captives up close. The villagers yelled at the two Americans, burned them with cigarettes, threw stones at them and kicked or hit them with sticks. Eventually, the haranguing stopped.

The weather was sweltering. After sunset, Ev and Jack, still tied and blindfolded, were again placed into the vehicle, and the journey to Hanoi continued under the cover of darkness and without benefit of headlights.

At some time late in the night, they entered Hanoi and were transported through the deserted, dark streets. The journey from the southern outskirts of Hanoi to the city center near Hoan Kiem Lake lasted perhaps not even an hour. Finally, the vehicle made one last turn onto a dark, short, deserted street not more than five hundred feet long that paralleled a long, high stone wall located to the right side. Soon thereafter, about two hundred fifty feet down the street, the vehicle turned right into a short driveway and stopped in front of a building and waited. No lights could be seen. Ev and Jack, blindfolded, weren't sure where they were although they knew they had come north from Thanh Hoa and were most likely in Hanoi. They also surmised they had probably arrived at a place they had only read or heard about but never dreamed they would visit.

A large *porte-cochere* with French doors that formed the main access to the building, in front of which the vehicle was parked, was located beneath a stone arch and a heavy grate of thick perpendicular steel bars. The doors were located roughly in the center of the long, imposing stone wall. The wall was topped with electrified wire and shards of colored, broken glass. A semi-circular array of capital letters carved in the arch above the doors read, "MAISON CENTRALE."

Soon, the clanking sound of metal shanks could be heard as the doors' locks were opened and removed from their latches. The thick French doors, their heavy iron hinges creaking, swung slowly inward and opened to reveal a dimly lit corridor—what looked to be a tunnel. Barely able to squeeze through the door opening, the military vehicle was driven into the tunnel that accessed a main foyer inside the dank interior of an ominous building and then stopped. The heavy doors closed behind the vehicle and were locked. Ev and Jack had arrived at Nha tu Hoa Lo, or Hoa Lo Prison, what the Americans called the "Hanoi Hilton."

Chapter 22

In the Grasp of Lilliputians: The *Con Ma* Is Moved

THE MORNING AFTER THE AMERICAN air strike on the Ham Rong Bridge, long before the sun rose and just after he had retired, Nguyen heard loud voices outside his home in the small crowded village. He rose from his narrow, matted cot and, pushing a curtain to one side, looked out the short, narrow door. A large crowd had gathered in front of his home. A man in uniform, an officer, approached him and, speaking rapidly and with authority, told him that the *may bay my* that had landed in the Song Ma must be moved and concealed immediately. He had heard that Nguyen had a barge and could make the necessary arrangements. Nguyen and some of his friends were now required to arrange for the transfer of the American plane from the point of an island in the Song Ma to another, more concealed place so that the plane might be examined in closer detail out of sight of the Americans and without risk of it being destroyed by them.

Nguyen agreed and said he would begin the task immediately. He thought back to the moment the plane had flown directly above his head and then later, how he and so many others had scrambled over it, some scratching their names and the date on the side of the plane where the two Americans had been seated. Nguyen's mind began to race: ropes, barges, pulleys, winches—all of these things; and people. He had a lot to organize. Although he had been up most of the night and had had little sleep, he immediately dressed and left home to begin preparations. He already had a plan but the ordeal would prove more difficult than he was to imagine. Only now did Nguyen realize the enormity of the officer's demand. He did not have a telephone but he was able to spread the news of his need for help to his contacts using the people in the village as runners.

Nguyen made his way across the mud flats toward the *may bay my*. The black-gray mud was as slippery as it had been the day before; as it always was. By the time he reached the *may bay my*, he was covered up to his waist in black, oozing, clinging mud. Nguyen walked around the Phantom, now camouflaged from sight. The tide had risen and fallen during the night. Mud crabs were crawling everywhere. The water level, now receded, had risen to almost half the height of the fuselage. The broad wings of the *may bay my*, resting on the mud, were now covered in river sludge. Nguyen, with increasing curiosity, eyed the ungainly, now impotent beast through the camouflage as the sun peeked over the horizon.

Nguyen took note again of the star and stripe emblem on the sides of the plane in front of the wings, the numbers on each side, "3001," the letter and number combination, "VF-114," the four letters on the side, "N-A-V-Y," and the two letters that were painted on the tail, "NH." He had no idea as to the significance of these letters or numbers. He had learned that the aircraft was an F-4 Phantom, a *Con ma*. But on this visit, Nguyen noticed writing he had not seen before: "USS KITTY HAWK." He had heard the plane had come from the sea but was not sure what those specific words meant. These letters piqued his interest. Nguyen examined the air giant in closer detail. There was so much about the aircraft that was mysterious. He noticed seven, much smaller letters written on the right side of the plane just in front of the air intake: "BAKER L.F." What could these small, solitary letters mean? What was their significance? Nguyen noted an orange stripe at the top of the tail fin at the back of the plane with some caricature painted in white. What did this symbolize? Nguyen continued to walk around the lifeless *Con ma* eyeing various mechanical intricacies. He stepped up onto its right wing, which lay flush with the ground. The wing was covered with a film of mud. Nguyen could still vaguely make out the same two large letters, "NH," painted in black on the wing's surface near the wing tip that he had observed on the tail fin. He saw three large numbers just to the left of the letters also painted in black that read "201." All these letters and numbers: surely they meant something. But what?

Nguyen looked into the front cockpit, now saturated with water, and pondered the gauges, dials, levers and intricate switches. He peered into the intakes and the rear of the engines. The plane held many fascinating puzzles that Nguyen knew would remain unsolved for the rest of his life. He was intrigued by this American military air machine, this silent giant that had fallen from the skies.

The thought or significance of what he had witnessed several hours before and was now seeing had not really sunk in. What he had experienced in the late afternoon the day before when the plane flew directly over his head was further augmented by the scale of the task given him and by the sheer physical presence of the American plane sitting in the mud before him. Nguyen was in awe. He knew he was standing next to and looking directly at a prize of war, a feared *Con ma*. Enough of this: he knew he had to move it. Time to get started.

Stragglers and those whose curiosity had not allowed them to sleep the night before lingered about; some were still talking excitedly. In spite of the presence of a few military people, a crowd had begun to gather again. A party atmosphere prevailed, but Nguyen paid no attention. He had a lot to do. Nguyen, having lit a cigarette, surveyed the area. Standing silently to one side and a little in front of the plane, as he inhaled and exhaled the cigarette smoke, he thought: moving this *may bay my* is going to be very tricky.

The only way to move the plane off the mud flats was either to drag it across the flats three hundred meters to the more firm embankment or to somehow tow it upstream to a place where it could be hauled up quickly on the riverbank. Although Nguyen knew that towing the plane downstream would be out of the question, neither of the other two options would be easy either. Of the two ideas, the least practical was winching it off the mud flats some three hundred meters to firmer land. The thick, saturated mud rendered this impossible. The area around the mud flats provided virtually no concealment so once the plane had been moved there, it would still be at risk of being destroyed by the Americans. This was clearly not the correct option.

Nguyen decided he would float the plane upstream to a point where he knew it could be beached, where the mud was not so hindering, and where the plane could be brought ashore and concealed. But how?

Nguyen had promised that the plane would be moved immediately. He had a lot of things to organize. He had made contact with all his friends. He arranged for many large and small barges, large winches and cable, jacks, large timbers, and his own much larger barge with a more powerful engine.

This was Nguyen's plan: At low tide he would dig beneath the wings to a depth that would allow for barges to be wedged beneath the wings of the *Con ma*. Nguyen enlisted the entire village to excavate beneath the wings. The barges would be flooded with water to allow them to sink and be towed into place. Cables and ropes would be placed at various points on the plane and attached to his barge that had an engine powerful enough to tow it. But his own barge would have to be positioned far in front of the *Con ma* in water deep enough that it could operate. Tricky again because that means the barge would be vulnerable to the river's flow. It would be hard to keep his barge stationary while everything was being hooked up. Once the water-filled barges were positioned beneath the wings, the water would be bucketed out. When the tide came in, the buoyancy of the barges would overcome the sucking mud and lift the plane. It would float. Once floating, even if partially submerged, the *Con ma* would be towed upstream, more or less to the northwest, to a landing site. It was an added benefit that the plane was already pointing in the direction in which it was about to be towed.

Nguyen knew of a perfect landing place for the aircraft about two or three kilometers upstream from the mud flats. From this point not more than two hundred meters ashore, he knew of a large, dense bamboo grove that would serve as the perfect concealment. He had sent one of his friends to take a look and report back. But to bring the *Con ma* to that location, Nguyen had to devise a rail-and-winch system to pull the plane up and out of the water and then into the grove some distance away.

For two days, there was a constant hubbub of activity both at the site of the *Con ma* and at its future resting place.

Because the main channel or the most easily navigable portion of the river was near the south side of the river, the trip upriver would be painfully slow and perilous. Any number of things could go wrong: The barges could sink or the American plane could fall off the barges, capsizing them, and be lost forever. The towing operation would begin just before the evening's high tide and would take several hours.

With more than a hundred people digging channels in the mud to the plane and beneath the wings in order to accommodate the smaller barges that sat sunk by their having been flooded, progress had been slow. Finally, the channels that had been dug to facilitate sliding the barges beneath the wings were complete. The barges were slid into place beneath the wings and emptied of the water that had been used to sink them. They were secured by rope around the wings. Cables were made ready to attach the *Con ma* to the towing barge.

The winch-and-pulley system at the landing site was made ready too. Knowing that at this location the bank of the river was about four or five feet above the waterline at high tide, workers prepared a ramp by shaving off the embankment with shovels in order to ease the *Con ma* from the water up and onto firm ground.

At 7:00 p.m. on the third night, as the tide was beginning to swell and fill the estuaries, the towing barge was positioned far in front of the *Con ma* and the cables attached.

Digging beneath the wings, workers discovered something very advantageous to their efforts. Beneath the fuselage and on each side where the wings connected to the plane, two steel hooks were already attached to the plane. How perfect! Cables were placed over the hooks. Little did the workers know these were the same hooks over which cables had been placed to launch Linfield Two Zero One from *Kitty Hawk*.

Everyone worked in total darkness. The water rose slowly and soon Nguyen heard creaks and moans as the buoyancy of the barges supporting the wings took over and began to lift the *Con ma* from the suction of the dense, airless mud. The towing barge took up the slack and the cable began to tighten. The height of the river increased and finally the *Con ma* broke free from the mud of the Song Ma and floated, but barely. There was very little freeboard.

Now for the hard part.

Cables from other smaller barges had been attached to Linfield Two Zero One and steadied the Phantom on each side. The towing barge began to inch forward upstream as the operator applied power to the engine—the towing cable tightened. The plane floated low. The supporting barges held and the plane rocked as waves splashed up its sides. The mud was washing away now and Nguyen saw the large black number again: *3001*. The operator of the towing barge applied more power and the engine strained against the load it was expected to bear upriver. The river current worked against the workers but there was no other option, no other place to take the *Con ma* that offered access to firmer ground or concealment.

The barges, their engines chugging under the strain, began to tow the *Con ma* upstream against the current. The plane moved steadily and relatively easily as waves slapped at its sides. Slowly, inexorably, the F-4 Phantom had begun its last journey, not proudly in the air, but sadly, on dilapidated wood barges up the Song Ma.

As a guide, the team at the receiving point placed small, dimly lit lanterns so as to allow the boatmen to maneuver their barges closer. The barges ran aground at the intended point about four hours later. Once the *Con ma* was secured to the bank, the barges were disconnected and other ropes and cables were attached to the Phantom. Another winch motor was started. With much difficulty, the Phantom was now dragged off the barges and then, inch by inch, jacked up onto a skid of large timbers that had been positioned ready for the plane. The fuselage rested on the skid and the skid rested on wood planking that would serve as a pathway along which the *Con ma* would be dragged. This activity consumed several hours.

The *Con ma* was winched slowly forward, first up the notch cut in the river bank and then along flat ground about two hundred meters toward a bamboo grove in an area next to a small farm building. The wood railings or planking were leap-frogged ahead of the Phantom each time it had passed a section. The giant American plane, with numbers and letters on its sides, moved not with grace but still with dignity. Its bearing and countenance were impressive to all who surveyed it. The *Con ma*, finally positioned within the bamboo grove, was camouflaged immediately.

Nguyen caught one last glimpse of the American warplane as workers scurried all over it placing vegetation on it. Soon the *Con ma* was totally concealed from view.

A silence fell upon the sweating workers as they realized the sheer size of the American aircraft and the magnitude of what they had accomplished. Nguyen was exhausted. He lit a cigarette and inhaled deeply. He had succeeded in accomplishing what even he had feared would be impossible. Once the job of moving the plane had been completed, he was no longer needed.

Over the next many days, Ev and Jack's Phantom would be examined by others, its systems dissected. At some point in time, it would be cut into pieces with cutting torches to facilitate its disembowelment and hauling. Nguyen never saw the *may bay my*, the *Con ma,* again and never knew what became of it.

Chapter 23
The Fate of the Thanh Hoa Bridge

THE U.S. NAVY STRIKE FROM *KITTY HAWK* on 14 May 1967 did not destroy the Thanh Hoa Bridge.

One year prior to the downing of Ev and Jack, the U.S. Air Force tried a novel way of destroying the Thanh Hoa Bridge. If it could not be blown up from above, perhaps it could be unhinged or blown up from below. To accomplish this, C-130s were used in a mission known as *Carolina Moon*. They carried specially developed bombs that, once dropped upstream of the Thanh Hoa Bridge, would float downstream. When their metal detectors picked up the "scent" of the steel trusses, the bombs would detonate.

The plan failed. On the second and last attempt, a C-130 was lost, its crew of eight killed. Years after the war, the remains of some of the crew were repatriated to the USA.

The Thanh Hoa Bridge seemed invincible, its destruction not possible. It withstood the American air onslaught until it was finally crippled and brought to its knees on 13 May of 1972. Laser-guided bombs dropped from U.S. Air Force F-4 Phantom IIs, the flight of which was led by Colonel Richard G. Horne, dislodged Nguyen Dinh Doan's bridge at Thanh Hoa from its western abutment, felling it into the muddy river below. The massive steel truss, bent and distorted, collapsed under the strain.

The exuberance of upper echelon U.S. planners remained unabated by this excellent result. Additional attacks were planned and executed against the Thanh Hoa Bridge.

The next day, on 14 May 1972—five years to the day after Ev and Jack were shot down over Thanh Hoa—General John Vogt issued the following communiqué:

From General Vogt to all who participated in yesterday's attack on the Thanh Hoa Bridge, I congratulate and commend each one of you for a most difficult and hazardous task well done....

Later, Colonel Horne, the flight leader, was to receive this commendation personally from General Vogt:

To Dick Horne;
An outstanding combat leader on this historic mission.
John W. Fogt

Dick Horne also received the Distinguished Flying Cross (Ninth Oak Leaf Cluster), the partial citation for which read, "COL Richard G. Horne distinguished himself by extraordinary achievement while participating in aerial flight as an F-4D Aircraft Commander near the Thanh Hoa Bridge."

In October 1972, a flight of four A-4 aircraft launched from a U.S. aircraft carrier. Escorted by flak suppression fighters, again F-4s, the A-4s dropped six 2,000-pound, laser-guided bombs on the structure, effectively putting the Thanh Hoa Bridge permanently out of commission.

Jack Rollins preparing to climb aboard Linfield Two Zero One of VF-114 prior to a mission over North Vietnam from the deck of the USS *Kitty Hawk* steaming in the Tonkin Gulf. Jack had previously been assigned to the Fleet Introduction Team for the F-4 Phantom II as a Radar Intercept Officer (RIO). He was then assigned to VF-114, the first F-4 Phantom II squadron. (Photo courtesy Jack Rollins)

Linfield Two Zero One of VF-114, Air Wing Eleven (CVW-11), off the USS *Kitty Hawk,* 1966-67 cruise to Vietnam. (Photo courtesy Isamu Yatsuhashi, from Jack Rollins collection)

Aerial view of the Song Ma and the Ham Rong Bridge (*center*) looking west. (U.S. Navy photo, courtesy Alexander Wattay)

The main bombing strike on the Ham Rong Bridge by Air Wing Eleven from the USS *Kitty Hawk*, 14 May 1967. (U.S. Navy photo, courtesy Alexander Wattay)

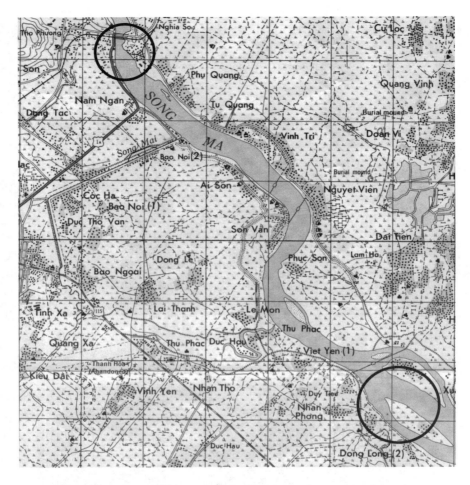

A North Vietnamese map showing Thanh Hoa and environs along the Song Ma (Ma River). The Thanh Hoa bridge crosses the Song Ma in an almost due east-west direction at a narrow isthmus near the top of the map.

The flight of Linfield Two Zero One ended just at the northwest tip of a small island in the Song Ma about seven kilometers southeast of Thanh Hoa (*bottom, right edge of map*). Ev Southwick was flying southeast when he and Jack Rollins ejected at about fifty or sixty feet above the ground. The Phantom continued southeast, hit the mud flats and ground looped (spun around) in the mud. It was from this location that the North Vietnamese towed the plane upstream to a bamboo grove for inspection

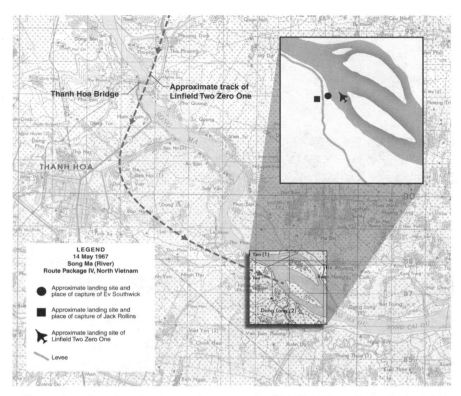

Illustration showing the approximate track of Linfield Two Zero One and the relative sites of Ev and Jack's capture, 14 May 1967

The grove of bamboo into which the North Vietnamese moved Linfield Two Zero One from the exposed mud flats of the Song Ma several kilometers downstream. Concealed from view, here the plane was dissected and its electrical/mechanical systems removed. The plane was moved to Hanoi in about 1985

By the time Sven Oste of *Dagens Nyheter* (a Swedish newspaper) arrived at the site on the Ma River around midnight on 14 May 1967, the tide in the estuary had risen to partially submerge the F-4 Phantom that was Linfield Two Zero One. Ev and Jack's Phantom landed southeast of Thanh Hoa off the tip of a small island in the tidal waters of the Song Ma not far from the coast. North Vietnamese villagers placed camouflage over some of the F-4 in an attempt to conceal it from the Americans. The RAT doors on the upper side of the fuselage are still open. The bureau number, air wing designation, squadron number, insignia, and the aardvark mascot symbol (at the top of the tail) are clearly visible. When Oste reported seeing the F-4 to U.S. officials in Hong Kong two days later, they were skeptical; until he told them about the markings and their juxtaposition on the plane and about the smaller letters and numbers barely seen to the right of the larger numerals 3001: F-4B 153001. He also told the American officials that the two airmen were unhurt but he didn't see them. He had heard that there were two planes shot down that day but he did not see the second plane. (Photo courtesy of Dagens Nyheter and Scanpix, Sweden)

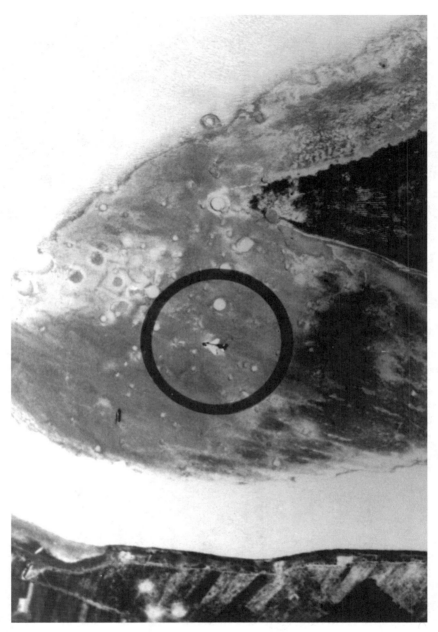

Aerial photo of the wreckage of Linfield Two Zero One taken sometime after the Phantom crashed in the Song Ma on 14 May 1967. Note the bomb craters as a result of the Navy's attempts to destroy the Phantom (Photographed by Alexander Wattay, U.S. Navy, photo courtesy Jack Rollins collection)

Linfield Two Zero One lies abandoned southeast of Thanh Hoa after being totally stripped of its systems (Photo courtesy Jack Rollins collection)

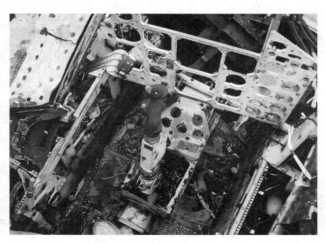

The front cockpit of Linfield Two Zero One in Hanoi. All instruments have been removed

The Thanh Hoa (Ham Rong) Bridge lies in ruin after having been destroyed by U.S. Air Force F-4s led by COL Richard G. Horne on 13 May 1972. Colonel Horne received the Distinguished Flying Cross as a result of this mission

A classic photograph of the Thanh Hoa Bridge, which was destroyed on 13 May 1972. Under the command of COL Richard G. Horne, a flight of U.S. Air Force F-4 Phantoms using lasar-guided bombs targeted the western abutment felling the western truss into the Song Ma (Photo courtesy Naval History and Heritage Command)

Post strike photograph showing damage to Thanh Hoa Railroad and Highway Bridge. October 6, 1972 (U.S. Navy photo, courtesy Naval History and Heritage Command)

Immediately after the war, the North Vietnamese began the reconstruction of Cau Ham Rong. Here, Nguyen Dinh Doan (*pointing with pen*) explains to his fellow engineers how he intends to re-construct the Ham Rong Bridge, which was finally destroyed by the Americans in May 1972 and attacked agin in October 1972. (Photo courtesy Nguyen Dinh Doan)

The wreckage of Linfield Two Zero One at the Air Defense Museum in Hanoi in 2004. The Phantom has been moved to the combined Air Defense/Air Force Museum on Truong Chinh Street, Thanh Xuan District, Hanoi. The RAT doors can still be seen in their open position

The Ram Air Turbine bay on the upper left side of the fuselage of the Phantom. The RAT is retracted but still visible

The bureau and squadron numbers are still visible on the wreckage of Linfield Two Zero One in Hanoi

A close-up of the wreckage shows what looks to be the name of the Plane Captain painted on the right fixed intake ramp. The Plane Captain is responsible for the operational readiness of the plane

Ev Southwick's control stick in the wreckage of Linfield
Two Zero One

The RAT lever located just to the left of Ev's left shoulder in the
front cockpit of the wreckage of the Phantom. Engaging this lever
activated the Ram Air Turbine which was an emergency generator

This crude model of the Thanh Hoa Bridge was constructed by a Vietnamese craftsman after the war to honor those who defended it and to depict its geographic layout and air defense. The model is placed on display and maintained by the little-known, seldom-visited Thanh Hoa Museum

Helmets, boots and other artifacts of U.S. airmen shot down in the vicinity of Thanh Hoa on display in the Thanh Hoa Museum. Neither the helmets of Ev Southwick and Jack Rollins nor their ejection seats were found

During the author's search for the landing spot of Linfield Two Zero One, he visited several villages along the Song Ma. Everyone knew the story of the *Con ma*. Individual recollections of the events of 14 May 1967 would often spark boisterous controversy, even heated debate, among the villagers. Wherever the author went, a noisy crowd would immediately gather. Everyone had a tale to tell as each person competed for attention and the bragging rights of relating the story of the *Con ma*

Author standing on the Ham Rong (or Thanh Hoa) Bridge, 2008. Banner reads: "Do Everything to Maintain Safety"

Chapter 24

Facing the Dragon: Ev and Jack Return to the Thanh Hoa Bridge

IT HAPPENS: SOONER OR LATER, we return to a place where an event occurred that had a significant impact on our lives, particularly if the event was a traumatic one. It seems an innate characteristic of the human being that we are consciously or unconsciously driven to relive a tragedy in our past and are drawn back to that locale. By facing the devil, so to speak, we help relieve ourselves of the memories of a trauma over which we had little control, of an event that was perhaps much larger than we but in which, even if in some small way, we nonetheless participated—like bit actors in some grand scheme. The phenomena cannot be so easily explained.

United States war veterans have returned to Normandy, Iwo Jima and Korea. At some point in the future, men and women will return to Iraq and Afghanistan. Many Americans who fought in the Vietnam War are now returning to Vietnam.

Ev Southwick and Jack Rollins had planned to return to Vietnam in 2003. However, because of the outbreak of a viral respiratory disease that began in Hong Kong and which evolved into the SAR epidemic that eventually afflicted much of Asia, they delayed their return until the following year. Ev and Jack returned to Vietnam in May 2004, a few days before the 37th anniversary of their shoot-down. This story cannot be told, it cannot reach conclusion, without an account of their return.

Ev and Jack left San Diego on or about 10 May and arrived at Noi Bai Airport, thirty-two kilometers from Hanoi, around noon on 12 May. The name Noi Bai was alien to them. They would have known the airport facilities thirty-seven years before by another name: Phuc Yen, an airbase for MiG fighter jets. MiGs are still based there. They were met at the airport by Hoang Tran Dung, who acted as their guide and interpreter during their return visit.

Hoang served in the *Quan Doi Nhan Dan Viet Nam*, (People's Army of Vietnam—PAVN) late in the Vietnam War, not as a direct combatant, but as an officer with the *bo doi thong tin*, or communications troops. He was stationed around Khe Sanh and Pleiku and entered Saigon the day the North Vietnamese toppled the South Vietnam government. But the war was far behind him now as he accompanied the two returning Americans and showed them around.

The day after their arrival, Ev and Jack visited Hoa Lo prison, now a museum. During the course of their captivity years earlier, Ev and Jack would be incarcerated in Hoa Lo and in other prisons in and around Hanoi and even as far north as the border with China. Each of them was imprisoned in North Vietnam for almost six years. They sometimes shared the same cell but otherwise they rarely saw each other over the subsequent years. They were not alone; their fate would be shared by several hundred other U.S. airmen. In the spring of 1973, the American POWs, Ev and Jack among them, would return to the United States from Hoa Lo and other prisons in North Vietnam.

Hoa Lo derives its name from a time long past when Vietnamese artisans manufactured small portable earthenware charcoal cooking stoves in the area where the French built their *Maison Centrale* (Central Prison). The Vietnamese name for these stoves is *hoa lo* (pronounced, wha law), which, when translated literally into English, means roughly "fiery oven." After independence, the Vietnamese renamed *rue de la Prison*, the street on which the prison sat, to *Pho Hoa Lo* (Hoa Lo Street) in recognition of the traditional local industry that once thrived there. *Pho Hoa Lo* is about five hundred feet long and is the only street in Hanoi with a single address: a single entrance to the collection of connected buildings which the French called *Maison Centrale* and the Vietnamese later named *Nha tu Hoa lo*, or in English, Hoa Lo Prison—what the American POWs dubbed the "Hanoi Hilton." During the time of the Vietnam War, of course, there was no Hilton Hotel in Hanoi but there is today—the Hilton Hanoi Opera Hotel.

Hoa Lo was as Ev and Jack had remembered it, but only to some degree. Rooms and cells had been changed, rearranged, lopped off, demolished, and removed altogether. The prison was cleaned up, the walls painted, the floors swept. The one-hundred-fifty-year-old French prison was a mere fifth, maybe less, of its original size.

When Ev and Jack arrived at the prison gates through which they entered in 1967, they stood outside the large *porte-cochere* doors and gazed at the tall outside wall of an imposing edifice they had previously seen only from the inside. Now with great humor, remembering that fateful night years ago when they had first entered the prison, each man, bowing and crossing his arms in front of his body in a mock welcome gesture, invited the other inside the prison gates.

Ev and Jack remembered the main entrance, the tunnel and the Knobby Room—a room so named because of nodules of plaster dotting the walls to muffle sounds that might escape from the room during onerous prisoner interrogation. The two American airmen were animated and curious about the facility. They looked around and talked to each other about the features of what they recalled. Once inside, they walked the dark hallways, visited the small cells and areas of the prison they knew, and scrutinized the displays of artifacts taken from other American airmen who had also been incarcerated there. But most of the areas they remembered, such as the large open space the POWs called "Unity," had been torn down to make way for twin high-rise buildings constructed on the same grounds.

The two airmen also visited what was left of another prison the American POWs called "The Zoo." The Zoo was an old French movie production center where Ev and Jack had spent many months. Since most of the buildings and structures had been razed and replaced, neither man was sure of the layout. Once Jack found the main entrance gate, still there at the time of their visit, the geographical layout of the prison immediately fell into place in his and Ev's minds. They recalled all the geographical characteristics of the make-shift prison facility.

While Ev and Jack found their visit to Hoa Lo and the remains of the Zoo interesting, their reunion with Linfield Two Zero One, their F-4B Phantom II aircraft, would be significant. They had seen their plane only in photographs.

Recently the Vietnamese consolidated two museums, the Air Force Museum and the Air Defense Museum (now called *Bao Tang Phong Khong Khong Quan*), at a nice, modern and well maintained facility in Hanoi. At the time of Ev and Jack's visit, these two museums, were separated by about a kilometer on the same street. At the then *Bao Tang Phong Khong* (Air Defense Museum) where their Phantom was on display beneath a large tree, the visit proved remarkable.

The main gates to the Air Defense Museum were open and Hoang drove into the premises stopping just inside the gate. Ev and Jack climbed out of the vehicle. Nguyen Anh, the director of the Air Defense Museum, through his aides, welcomed the two Americans to his museum. Ev and Jack walked a little forward and then looked to the right. They saw a MiG-21 and a surface-to-air missile on display. An array of green antiaircraft weaponry could be seen to their left. But directly in front of them sitting amid a pile of airplane wreckage, the real reason why they visited the museum was revealed.

The mutilated remains of Linfield Two Zero One, elevated and slanted on a steel and concrete frame, sat patiently, as if waiting for its two occupants to return to claim their plane. Both men stopped for a second and stared at the Phantom. The gray and white paint of so long ago, had turned a greenish hue. The vertical tail fin was torn leaving only a stub. The canopies were long gone. The nose as well as the rear wings, technically referred to as stabilators, were missing. A few panels dangled beneath the fuselage and swung on their hinges. The engines were no longer in their positions and the skin was punctured in many places resulting in large gapping or jagged holes in the fuselage. Yet, for all this, the Phantom was still recognizable.

Ev and Jack, being mindful of the rough, dangerous debris strewn haphazardly about, walked closer to the F-4. Each airman peered into the cockpit just at shoulder level and walked all around the big plane. Ev was animated about what he was seeing. He pointed out so many small aspects of the plane as he recounted out loud what he could recall about it. He noted all the instruments were gone. He saw that the main landing gears were still in their retracted position, the RAT doors open, and the RAT handle and the control stick still in place.

Ev and Jack, now standing beneath the empennage, peered up into the nacelle where the engines would have been and noticed the scorching the inside of the skin of the fuselage had received from the hot temperatures generated by the engines. They looked at the still-intact engines, sitting in front of the Phantom that had been damaged by shrapnel.

At the end of Ev and Jack's museum visit and just before they left, they were invited into the office of Nguyen Anh. The square office was not large. It contained small wood chairs and a small table for guests and a much larger desk for the curator. Tea was brought in and offered to the two returning Americans. Nguyen Anh was pleased to meet Ev and Jack. For the first time in his life, he met the two men who occupied the F-4 that could have been considered the centerpiece of his military artifact collection. Mr.

Anh was curious about the plane and its occupants as he had very little information about either. He asked many questions.

The visit to the Air Defense Museum and Linfield Two Zero One was successful and fascinating and yet, since the two airmen would again abandon their Phantom, a little sad.

One last destination remained.

The day, 14 May 2004, had begun ominously enough: heavy clouds hung over Hanoi and the streets were damp from a light rain that had fallen in the predawn hours. Hanoi was its usual dark self. Lit intermittently by small lights suspended over the streets and intersections, the outlines of trees and buildings, even the curbs themselves could barely be discerned. The streets were quiet. Only the sound of a lone bicycle rattling along the wet street could be heard as the bicyclist, legs pumping, rotated its pedals. The hotel where Ev and Jack stayed was (and is) located adjacent to the opulent opera house not even a mile from Hoa Lo, the infamous prison dubbed the Hanoi Hilton.

On this date, on exactly the thirty-seventh anniversary when Ev and Jack were shot down, the two Americans would return to the Thanh Hoa Bridge, as they knew the name, just northwest of Thanh Hoa and visit the site where their luck had run out so many years earlier. The early morning hours of 14 May held the promise of great discovery, remembrances, and adventure. The day would surely prove to be as fascinating as their reunion with their Phantom.

After eating bowls of *pho* (noodle soup), a typical Vietnamese breakfast, in a tiny restaurant not far from the hotel, accompanied by Hoang Tran Dung, Ev and Jack left Hanoi just after sunrise and made their way south in a comfortable, air-conditioned van on National Highway Number 1. Destination: Thanh Pho Thanh Hoa (Thanh Hoa City). The weather, with its overcast of low, dark clouds and sporadic drizzle, did not bode well for the visitors that day. The humidity was stifling.

As Ev and Jack traveled south, toward Ninh Binh, the skies darkened and the clouds dropped lower. It was going to rain; and rain it did. Still, with some distance to go to reach Thanh Hoa, perhaps the sky would become clearer; but at the moment the weather was not cooperating.

Proceeding past Ninh Binh, Ev and Jack saw a red and white road marker on the right side of the road that read: "Ham Rong," in black letters, and below the inscription, "22 Km." The two U.S. Navy airmen were about to see for themselves the bridge that they and others collectively had tried to destroy decades before. Ev and Jack had no real perspective of the geographic layout from the vantage of ground level. They did not know what to look for or where the bridge could first be seen from the road.

The dark clouds began slowly to lift by mid-morning; visibility began to improve. The van turned off the newly realigned Highway 1 onto the old highway and ambled through a small cluster of low-lying buildings and crowded, wet streets. Ev and Jack had reached Ham Rong village—the road sign said so. Although the area was wet, there was little hint of rain now, a welcome relief from what the weather had presented earlier that morning and through which they had just driven.

Nui Ngoc, or Jade Hill, with its tall flagpole firmly placed in its concrete foundation on top, was in plain sight. In the slightly foggy, late morning, the van, slowing to a crawl, approached the east side of the Ma River.

There, looming before the two American naval airmen, glaring at them in silence was the fabled Thanh Hoa Bridge, rebuilt after the war but now a rusting steel skeleton. Ev and Jack had arrived to personally visit the infamous bridge in Route Package IV, North Vietnam.

The darkened steel of the bridge stood out starkly against the soft grayness of the sky. There it was; the very bridge that defied American attacks. The same truss configuration, the same alignment, the same abutments, the same railway, the same muddy river and the same two hills that form the jawbone of the dragon on either bank; excepting the triple-A gun emplacements, it was all there.

The bridge filled the windscreen of the van. The van stopped short of the bridge approach at the base of Nui Ngoc. Ev and Jack were seeing from the ground the very bridge they had seen only from the air. The bridge sat lifeless, unpretentious; its surroundings silent and harmless.

No rain, but the air remained heavy with humidity. Ev and Jack emerged from the van a little confused about directions—easily understood given the geographic orientation of the bridge. The highway runs north-south but the bridge crosses the Ma River virtually due east-west.

Ev and Jack glanced all about them. They had never seen the bridge so close. Now, standing just a hundred feet north (east) of the bridge, they discussed the attack and where it had come from. Ev needed to see a map, which was retrieved from the van. Then, with a gesture, his bearings collected, Ev, looking up and around, said, *"We came from there and we passed*

Ev Southwick (*left*) and Jack Rollins visiting Hanoi, May 2004

Ev Southwick visits with some American tourists at Hoa Lo Prison in Hanoi, May 2004

Jack Rollins standing on the grounds of a prison (formerly an old French film studio) the American POWs called "the Zoo" in Hanoi, May 2004. Jack spent most of his POW years at the Zoo. The only thing remaining of the old prison today is the main entrance gate

Jack Rollins looks at a map of North Vietnam at the Army Museum in Hanoi, May 2004

Ev and Jack in front of the main door to Hoa Lo Prison in Hanoi, May 2004. Although Ev and Jack spent much of their captivity here, they were also held prisoners at other prison locations in North Vietnam

Entrance to Hoa lo Prison, the infamous "Hanoi Hilton." These are the same prison doors through which Ev and Jack and about six hundred fifty other Americans passed after their capture. It was also from these same doors that the American POWs would emerge when they were finally repatriated to the United States in the spring of 1973, Ev and Jack among them. In the case of Ev and Jack, the intervening time between capture and release was not quite six years. Put in a different context, while some American POWs experienced more or less, Ev and Jack spent six Christmases in the prisons of North Vietnam

Ev (*right*) and Jack survey the remains of Linfield Two Zero One in Hanoi, May 2004

Ev and Jack examining the remains of Linfield Two Zero One in Hanoi, May 2004

Jack Rollins (*left*) and Ev Southwick (*right*) with author next to
Linfield Two Zero One in Hanoi, May 2004

With a touch of ironic humor, Ev (*left*) and Jack stand beneath a sign welcoming visitors to Thanh Hoa, located on the west side of the Thanh Hoa Bridge, on 14 May 2004–thirty-seven years to the day after their fateful mission to destroy the flak sites near the bridge. In 1967, Ev, Jack and their Phantom were most unwelcome guests

Ev and Jack at the Thanh Hoa (Ham Rong) Bridge, 14 May 2004

From left to right: Jack Rollins, Ev Southwick, Hoang Tran Dung (guide and translator) and a photographer for *An Ninh* (Security) newspaper, on the Thanh Hoa Bridge, 14 May 2004

Ev Southwick and Hoang Tran Dung raise their glasses of *Bia Hoi* in a toast in the home of Ngo Thi Tuyen, Thanh Hoa, 14 May 2004

From left to right: Ev Southwick, Ngo Thi Tuyen, in her uniform, and Jack Rollins outside Tuyen's home in Thanh Hoa. For her actions at the Thanh Hoa Bridge during the Vietnam War, Tuyen received the official title of "Heroine"

Ev Southwick (*right*) with the son of the man (*center*) who captured him on 14 May 1967. The man on the left, who was much younger at the time, witnessed Ev's capture

Jack Rollins near where he landed and was captured on 14 May 1967

On the 37th anniversary of their capture, Ev and Jack take one last moment to reminisce before leaving the site where they were captured downstream of Thanh Hoa on 14 May 1967

Ham Rong Bridge on the Song Ma today with Nui Ngoc (Jade Mountain) in the background. The bridge is no longer used for major vehicle traffic and serves only the local population and the railroad. Photographed by Hoang Tran Dung

Ham Rong Bridge today as seen from downstream

View of the Ham Rong Bridge looking east along the railway through the truss. Nui Ngoc is to the right. The numbers "19-5" at the top represent Ho Chi Minh's birthday and the date of the inauguration of the second Ham Rong Bridge. The railway is inspected and its gauge measured on a frequent and regular basis

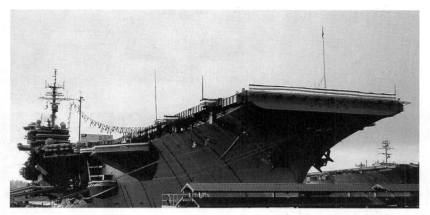

USS *Kitty Hawk* (CV-63), decommissioned in Bremerton, Washington, January 2009

USS *Kitty Hawk*, looking across the flight deck obliquely forward, toward the ship's island

Air Wing Eleven's six aerial combat kills during the Vietnam War are proudly displayed by red silhouettes of enemy aircraft on the starboard side of the island of *Kitty Hawk*. All kills were by F-4 Phantom IIs. From the bottom up, the symbols represent two AN-2 Colts shot down by Denny Wisely/David Jordan (VF-114) and David McRae/Dave Nichols (VF-213) in December 1966; two MiG-17s, shot down by Ev Southwick/Jim Laing and Denny Wisely/Gary Anderson (both of VF-114) in April 1967; and two MiG-21s shot down by Robert Hughes/Joe Cruz and Pete Pettigrew/Mike McCabe (both of VF-114) in May 1972

Author with the wreckage of Linfield Two Zero One at the Air Force/Air Defense Museum in Hanoi, Vietnam, 2009

Side view of Linfield Two Zero One wreckage

Wreckage of Linfield Two Zero One in Hanoi
Inset: Close-up of the plane's damaged right engine

An F-4 Phantom II in the markings of squadron VF-21 (Freelancers) (BuNo 153016) on display at the museum of the Arizona Wing of the Commemorative Air Force, Mesa, Arizona

186

An F-4 Phantom II on the flight deck of the USS *Midway* Museum in San Diego, California. This F-4 bares a different marking scheme for VF-21. Ev Southwick, who served on the *Midway*, volunteers as a docent aboard the now floating museum and gives lectures about launches and landings (traps) aboard an aircraft carrier

An operational F-4 Phantom II of the U.S. Air Force 20th Fighter Squadron (Silver Lobos), 49th Fighter Wing, from Holloman Air Force Base, at the annual air show in Oshkosh, Wisconsin in 2002. This F-4 was flown at that time by Mike Wilburn and Alex Mangold. The F-4 was phased out a few years later

AN F-4 Phantom II belonging to the Missouri Air National Guard placed on proud display atop a steel support pedestal at Lambert Field, St. Louis. This Phantom, originally manufactured on the other side of the runway, is credited with two MiG kills during the Vietnam War

An F-4 Phantom II, belonging to the U.S. Air Force Museum at Wright-Patterson Air Force Base, Dayton, Ohio, No longer a front line, state-of-the-art jet fighter, now retired, it takes its place prominently among the collection of other U.S. military aircraft and is an icon of historic airplane designs

The Collings Foundation's privately-owned F-4D Phantom II at Ellington Field, Texas; fully restored and completely operational. Painted in the colors and markings of the F-4 flown by the late then U.S. Air Force COL Robin Olds, the Phantom is used for flight demonstrations and displayed at air shows across the United States. This particular Phantom (USAF s/n 65-749, now registered as NX749CF) is credited with one MiG kill during the Vietnam War

An F-4N Phantom II (Bureau No.153915) bearing the markings of VF-154 (Black Knights) of Air Wing Fourteen (CVW-14) off the USS Coral Sea on proud display at the National Naval Aviation Museum at the U.S. Naval Air Station in Pensacola, Florida

189

An F-4 Phantom II (with landing gears extended) on display at the entrance to Battleship Memorial Park, Mobile, Alabama

The author's father, John Foster, standing next to an F-4 located at the Pima Air and Space Museum in Tucson, Arizona. He was a design and test engineer for McDonnell-Douglas Corp. and worked on aspects of the B-47, B-66, A-4, F-4, DC-9 and DC-10 aircraft

Author standing next to a discarded and abandoned partial F-4 Phantom II fuselage, Tucson, Arizona

It was in these facilities, located on the north side of Lambert Airfield in St. Louis, Missouri, that McDonnell Aircraft Company, under the direction of Herman D. Barkey, designed and manufactured the F-4 Phantom II. Today, the facilities are abandoned, the buildings empty, the gates locked, the area eerily quiet and lonely

Jack Rollins (*left*) and Ev Southwick in southern California today. Both men retired from the U.S. Navy and went on to lead successful careers in the private sector. Now fully retired, Ev and Jack enjoy time with their families, playing golf and taking a fishing trip together to southeast Alaska each year *through here and out,"* his arms pointing in a sweeping motion generally from north to south. *"We began having problems here,"* he said as he pointed to the sky. *"The flak was so dense there was a layer of smoke like a big, black cloud."*

The decaying, rusting, skeletal silhouette of the aging steel bridge had not changed in shape from when Ev and Jack had made their ill-fated visit to it as part of a U.S. naval air strike almost four decades before. Quiet and inert in its somewhat intrusive presence, the structure the Vietnamese call Cau Ham Rong, the aging pride of Thanh Hoa, rebuilt after the war, still spanned the Song Ma.

Seeing the bridge, neither Ev nor Jack was so sure now what all the fuss was about so many years before. Standing not far from the east abutment, just below Nui Ngoc, Ev, wearing sunglasses and face to face with the same bridge the defenses of which he targeted for destruction many years earlier, was not overly impressed with the size of the stationary structure. It didn't seem so awesome to either of the two returning U.S. Navy airmen. Jack, surveying the muddy water upstream and down, remembered the river being much wider as it sliced through the gorge.

Because of their collective memories and the seeming significance of the bridge that existed a long time ago, both Ev and Jack were expecting to see a much larger bridge, the size of which might span, say, the Mississippi River in the United States. They both had expected the bridge to be much larger, the river much wider.

Walking around on the ground, with glances toward the bridge and up onto the craggy hills that once bristled with antiaircraft defenses, one has to wonder why such a bridge, not a relatively large bridge, across such a river, not a particularly significant river, could assume such importance that obliged the U.S. Navy and U.S. Air Force to send strike aircraft to attack so often, only to lose so many expensive airplanes and their priceless pilots and crews.

Both airmen walked to the edge of the road near the approach to the bridge and peered down into the muddy eddies that swirled below.

Ev and Jack walked onto the structure itself. A few trucks passed over it on the cantilevered roadway, causing the rickety handrails, the exposed deck planking and the steel I-beams of the bridge superstructure to vibrate and rattle. The old, corroded steel rivets and bolts, having worked loose over the years, tenuously held the rusting steel members together.

They saw two numbers at the top of the truss on each entrance to the bridge: "19-5." The day and the month were auspicious as 19 May was not only Ho Chi Minh's birthdate (5-19-1890), it was also the same date on which he personally dedicated the Ham Rong Bridge in 1964 (which is what the numbers signify). And years later in 1967, the 19th of May was the worst day for the United States in the air war against North Vietnam.

Ev and Jack took pictures. In all, they were probably at the bridge site for less than thirty minutes. They were then driven to the other side of the bridge where they parked just below Nui Rong (Rong Mountain), the other jaw bone of the Dragon. Ev and Jack posed for photos beneath a sign that read "*Welcome to Thanh Hoa*," an ironic greeting for the two Americans who, many years before, had been most unwelcome and most unexpected guests there.

A slight rain began to fall.

Hoang Tran Dung took them to the home of Ms. Ngo Thi Tuyen. During the air war, Tuyen became the personified Vietnamese symbol of the struggle against the Americans, especially at the Thanh Hoa Bridge. She is known locally and nationally—and these are her official titles—as the Heroine of Ham Rong Bridge, or the Heroine of Thanh Hoa. Tuyen became famous for carrying heavy 57mm and heavier 85mm antiaircraft shells, two of which weighed almost as much as she did, to antiaircraft sites during American air strikes against the bridge.

Ev and Jack's van was parked at the front gate of Tuyen's small, narrow house. Hoang knocked on the door. He was told that she was not at home but was not far away, probably visiting neighbors next door. Ev and Jack were asked to enter her home and invited to sit in the living room. They were served tea. Tuyen's living room, typical of a Vietnamese house, was not more than thirteen feet square. Everything happens in that room. There was limited space but still room for motorcycles and bicycles, in addition to furniture.

An ensemble of two opposing couches separated by a low lying table was positioned against one wall. At the end of the room opposite the front door, a large cabinet filled with knickknacks, photos, and a few cups and glasses stood against the wall. A large picture of an Alps mountain scene, perhaps Switzerland, hung on one wall above one of the couches, while on the opposite wall pictures of Tuyen and her husband, both in uniform, had been placed above eye level. Ev and Jack sat down on the same couch while Hoang stood outside smoking a cigarette Both men remained quiet.

Tuyen entered her house and immediately shook the hand of each air-man excitedly, telling them they were welcome in her home. Tuyen ordered her grandchild to bring some *Bia Hoi*, a locally brewed beer, for the two Americans and when it came she filled their glasses to the brim. She wanted to toast new, good friends. Ev toasted and then sipped the not-so-bad, ice-diluted beer.

Ev, Jack, Hoang and Tuyen talked for about ten minutes. Hoang ex-plained to her that Ev and Jack flew the Phantom that had landed in the Song Ma. Tuyen remembered the story of the *Con ma* and again welcomed the two returning American airmen.

All of a sudden, Tuyen disappeared only to reappear a few minutes later dressed entirely in her military uniform replete with about twelve medals and ribbons. She wanted to have her photograph taken with the two Amer-ican airmen. Ev and Jack agreed and soon, photo after photo was taken. But time was slipping away. If Ev and Jack were to see the place where they ejected, they had to move on. They needed plenty of time to visit the site where the F-4 had landed and to try to find where they, themselves, fell to earth and were captured.

Ev and Jack, having said their goodbyes to the Heroine of Thanh Hoa, loaded back into the van. The van turned onto the main boulevard and was driven back north through the main street of Thanh Hoa, toward the new concrete bridge downstream from the rusting steel truss work of the Thanh Hoa Bridge. Hoang knew the exact location where the Phantom had landed but he was uncertain how to return there except by one route only: the river levee road. Hoang found the up-sloping entrance to the levee road and, turning right at the top, proceeded along the muddy road downstream. The going was tedious and at times very rough. The bumpy road was unpaved and really more of a trail. But the distance was only about five kilometers.

The sun peeked through the clouds, which eventually lifted and dissi-pated. The day would be salvaged after all. The temperature had risen to near ninety-five degrees and the humidity remained sweltering. The rice fields were very green, the area very tranquil; not a sound could be heard. Hoang stopped the van. He pointed east across a narrow channel to the tip of a treeless island, to a large expanse of flat, dark-gray mud: the tidal flats.

"*This where fenton jet land down*," Hoang said. Hoang continued to point to the location.

Ev and Jack piled out of the vehicle.

Maps and aerial photos, taken many years before, pinpointed the exact location. Hoang had indicated correctly where the *Con ma* had hit the mud. Ev and Jack were stepping back into history.

Jack spoke: "*I remember the trees passing by us on both sides. We were at or just below treetop level when Ev told me to eject. I pulled the ejection handle from between my knees. The next thing I knew, I was out of the cockpit.*"

Ev recalled seeing trees on each side of the F-4. It would be difficult for anyone other than a pilot to imagine the Phantom at treetop level at two hundred miles per hour, and that Ev and Jack were so close to disaster.

Jack was under the impression that the trees may have been as high as a hundred feet. But in reality the trees topped out at about sixty feet. The tallest trees in the areas were eucalyptus trees. The vegetation and foliage Ev and Jack saw on the day of their return visit were probably typical of what was around in 1967.

Some pieces of the mystery of the last moments of the flight of Linfield Two Zero One were beginning to come together. Both Ev and Jack recalled a levee large enough to support a road on top. The levee they were standing on was the only levee in the area, and it was visible in the 1967 aerial photographs.

Just prior to ejecting, Ev had been making for a wide spot in the river. After having passed over and a little east of Thanh Hoa, his heading was more or less southeast. Ev stayed with the aircraft, valiantly struggling to reach the river, until he was so close to the ground that he had no option but to eject. It was only at the very last second that first Jack (backseat first) and then Ev ejected. The F-4, being only about fifty feet above the ground when its crew ejected, streaked to the river in a southeasterly direction and a few seconds later slammed into the mud. There was no explosion and no fire after the crash.

Ev scanned the landscape and after reorienting the geography in his mind, he recalled that he landed on the river side of the levee in the flood plain, close enough to the river to see it clearly. Although he landed in a banana grove, he recalled that he had an unobstructed view of the river.

Jack knew that he had landed in a rice paddy, only then to realize, on the opposite side of the levee from where Ev had landed. There was no way of knowing exactly where he hit the ground.

As Ev and Jack surveyed the site in a relaxed manner, a crowd was gathering around them. They continued talking at length about where they were.

Ev walked toward the river to a point off the levee and stood to look at the area where he surmised he may have landed. He may have been standing on the very spot where he landed thirty-seven years earlier.

Jack remained uncertain as to exactly where he had landed, but he knew he was close to the location.

Then, an incredible thing happened.

Chapter 25
Ev and Jack's Captors

AN OLD MAN WAS WALKING ALONG the levee toward the congregation that had assembled around Ev and Jack. Considering his advanced age and the fact that he may have lived here all his life, Hoang asked the man if he remembered events associated with the Phantom or the two airmen years ago. He did! The Vietnamese man told Ev and Jack everything that he remembered. Hoang translated.

"*One pilot landed there*," he said, pointing to where Ev, quite by chance, had been standing near the river. "*And one pilot landed there*," he added, as he turned and pointed toward a rice paddy behind them.

Although neither Ev nor Jack knew it thirty-seven years earlier, they had landed within several hundred feet of each other.

"*The pilot who landed there* [in the rice paddy] *was stabbed and the knife remained in him*," the man said.

"*Where?*" Hoang asked in Vietnamese.

"*In the shoulder*," the man said, raising up his left arm and pointing to his right shoulder. "*The Con ma landed over there*," he said, pointing to the exact spot that had been conclusively identified from the aerial photographs.

Then another, younger man spoke up and said his father had stabbed one airman and left the knife in his right shoulder. He said he remembered the story. That was Jack! No one could have contrived this story so coincidentally or accurately.

The old man remembered that the Americans had tried to bomb the plane but never hit it. Then one day, the plane was gone. It had been removed from the mud flats. That's all he knew.

Jack remembered a few things. He landed in the mud on his back and was immediately submerged. After he had kicked himself to the surface, he recalled seeing what he thought was his parachute lying next to him. The parachute never opened. He was impressed with how neatly it had been folded. Then he recalled that the militia arrived as he was being stabbed. They must have come from the nearby village.

Coincidentally, a younger man wearing a T-shirt talked about the incident and after some discussion, Hoang realized that this was the son of the man who had captured Ev! The story he told was very close to what Ev remembered; this could not have been made up. He explained that his father had died many years ago at the age of eighty-five.

There it was: Ev and Jack were standing now at the exact location of the Phantom's crash site and the location of the two Navy airmen's landing spots in Route Package IV, North Vietnam, thirty-seven years earlier to the exact day, and, as luck would have it, almost to the exact hour!

Hoang became more animated. He turned to Ev and Jack and in his imprecise English said, "*This too interesting! Interesting too much!*"

Ev said, "*It's well after three p.m. If we want to get back to Hanoi before nightfall, we better get going.*"

He was right and it's true: if there is no need to be on Vietnam's highways at night, it is much better not to be. They had to go. Their stay on the same levee that existed at the time they were shot down, on the banks of the Song Ma, lasted about an hour.

Back in the van, the talk was lively. Hoang, now knowing his bearings, knew the correct road to take back to Thanh Hoa. The van would proceed upriver on the levee road to a small village named Le Mon and turn left. Instead of continuing on the levee road, Hoang drove around a small building in the middle of the road and passed straight through the small town. Once he gained the main road back to Thanh Hoa, Ev agreed this was the better of the two routes. He confidently surmised that this was the road they were forced to take as they began their trek to Hanoi in 1967. They drove over the new concrete bridge that spanned the Song Ma. To their left, Ev and Jack saw for the last time the Thanh Hoa Bridge

On the way back to Hanoi, Ev and Jack talked and reminisced about their capture. This was a historic drive for Ev and Jack, because thirty-seven years before, the two Navy airmen from VF-114, from *Kitty Hawk*, then newly captured POWs, bloodied, bound, blindfolded and placed in the back of a military vehicle, were forced to make this same journey on Highway 1. Jack recalled stopping in one place before reaching Hanoi where both men were put on public display. The most likely place for this to have occurred was near Phu Ly or Ninh Binh. Ev and Jack were transiting through the towns again.

The trip to Hanoi this time was much different from their first one many years ago; obviously more appealing and comfortable. As the sun descended to the horizon, the rice fields turned a sharp, translucent, brilliant green that is so typical of Vietnam's coastal plains.

The day had been a success. Ev and Jack arrived in Hanoi just after dark—safely off the dangerous highway and onto the city's bustling streets. That night, they enjoyed the comfort of their hotel, a *real* Hilton—not a dirty, clammy, disease-ridden, rat-infested prison—and partook of a sumptuous meal.

Ev and Jack had visited museums, Hoa Lo, the remains of their Phantom, the Thanh Hoa Bridge and the place where they were captured. They met many people including the families of the people who had captured them. A successful trip in every regard, Ev and Jack would make the most of their remaining time in Vietnam and explore Hanoi and take a day-long cruising house boat trip on Ha Long Bay. Their trip to Vietnam was almost over. They could just relax without being on a time table. They left Vietnam for the second time in their lives on 18 May 2004. Neither Ev nor Jack would probably ever return.

Chapter 26
Life Moves On: Ev, Jack and Others Today

WHAT BECAME OF EV SOUTHWICK AND JACK ROLLINS after their capture? Many accounts exist of the severe hardships, deprivations and horrors that American POWs experienced in North Vietnam's prisons. One only has to read these accounts to gain an appreciation of what Ev and Jack suffered after their capture. Yet it is impossible for anyone who was not there to truly know and understand the facts or to fathom the experience.

Ev and Jack rarely saw each other while in captivity. Both men's wounds healed over time but to this day both bear the scars of the ejection and their later treatment while in prison. Along with the other POWs, both airmen were released from prison by the North Vietnamese and repatriated to the United States in the spring of 1973.

After repatriation, Ev was admitted to Hastings College of the Law (University of California) in San Francisco. He graduated with a Juris Doctor degree in May 1976, and executed orders to the Navy Office of Legislative Affairs, Washington, D.C. Ev retired from active military duty as a Navy captain in the fall of 1977. With the exception of a one-year break in 1980 working for Jim Ellis, California state assemblyman and then senator, Ev spent the next ten years representing several corporations to the U.S. Congress.

In 1987, Ev was appointed Deputy Assistant Administrator for Congressional Relations at NASA headquarters in Washington, D.C, and retired from NASA in October of 1993. He moved to San Diego in January 1994. In 1995-96, he served on the staff of San Diego Mayor Susan Golding, and in 1997-98, on the district staff of Congressman Brian Bilbray.

Ev is now fully retired but performs various volunteer activities. He proudly serves as a member of the Board of Directors of the San Diego Air and Space Museum and as a docent aboard the USS *Midway* Museum, which is permanently moored in San Diego harbor. Ev has four children, three boys and a girl, and six grandchildren (five boys and a girl). He is currently unmarried.

Ev's military awards include the Silver Star, Legion of Merit, Distinguished Flying Cross, Bronze Stars, Air Medals, two Purple Hearts, the Prisoner of War Medal, and numerous campaign medals.

Jack Rollins returned to flying after his release from prison and was assigned to Squadron VF-121. He retired with the rank of commander from the U.S. Navy in 1977.

After retiring from the Navy, Jack worked in the aerospace industry as a management consultant and as a professor of business and management at various universities in southern California. He earned a Bachelor of Arts degree in history from the University of California at San Diego, a Master of Arts degree in education from Pepperdine University in southern California, and a Doctorate degree in business from the United States International University. Jack is fully retired and lives with his wife, Connie.

Jack's military awards include two Silver Stars, the Legion of Merit, two Distinguished Flying Crosses, three Bronze Stars, seven Air Medals, two Purple Hearts, three Navy Commendation Medals, the Prisoner of War Medal, three Good Conduct Medals, and numerous campaign medals.

Both men now live in southern California and enjoy golf and other activities when they can. Each year, during late summer, Ev and Jack make a trip together to Sitka in Southeast Alaska to fish for Salmon.

Others

Herman D. Barkey, chief design engineer of the F-4 Phantom II, *"Phather of the Phantom,"* is deceased. He is survived by his daughter, Bonnie Barkey Moore who lives near St. Louis.

David Lewis, also a key designer of the F-4 Phantom II, is deceased.

Sven Oste, journalist working for *Dagens Nyheter*, is deceased.

Ngo Thi Tuyen lives with her husband not far from the center of the city of Thanh Hoa.

Hoang Tran Dung lives with his wife and young child in Hanoi. His first son, Hieu, attends university in Canada.

Nguyen Minh Huan and Ho Van Phong, now quite elderly, live near the coast in Thanh Hoa Province.

Nguyen Dinh Doan retired from government service as a structural/construction engineer and lives in Hanoi.

Squadron VF-114 (the Aardvarks) continued its deployments to Vietnam to the end of the Vietnam conflict, registering many enemy aircraft shot down. The Aardvarks flew the F-4 Phantom II until 1975 when it transitioned to the now-retired F-14 Tomcat. Having received many recognitions and awards during its renowned service, VF-114 ceased flight operations at the end of November 1992 and was decommissioned in April 1993. A website, created by George Jones in honor of his father, LT George D. Jones, who was a former pilot with VF-114 and was killed in a catapult accident in an F-4 Phantom II off the USS *America* (CV-66) in the Mediterranean Sea in 1967, honors and preserves the squadron's long, colorful and distinguished history. Please visit *www.VF-114.org.*

Chapter 27

Silent Remnants of War: The Thanh Hoa Bridge, USS *Kitty Hawk,* the Remains of Linfield Two Zero One and the F-4 Phantom II

THE VIETNAM WAR RESULTED IN COLOSSAL LOSSES. North Vietnam conquered South Vietnam. The re-unification of the two countries that Ho Chi Minh sought became a reality. The Americans withdrew. But immediate peace did not reign. Conflicts still raged in Southeast Asia. The Socialist Republic of Vietnam found itself in irritating, less significant military actions against Cambodia, a country they occupied for a short while, and with China over what to some seemed like silly border disputes.

Rebuilding the infrastructure of Vietnam north of the 17th parallel became a national priority. Begun in 1973, the rebuilding effort proved tedious and costly. The north-south railway, Highway No. 1 between Hanoi and Ho Chi Minh City, Highway No. 5 between Hanoi and Haiphong and Highway No. 9 between Dong Ha and Khe Sanh, as well as thousands of bridges and culverts and many other elements of the country's infrastructure, were repaired, reconstructed or replaced altogether. A slow process, the reconstruction of the infrastructure and subsequent upgrades would continue into the 21st century.

The bent and twisted frame of the Thanh Hoa Bridge, *Cau Ham Rong,* lay in the Song Ma for many months after the war. It had to be rebuilt. The Vietnamese government turned again to Nguyen Dinh Doan, its famous engineer, who would inspect the destroyed structure in what he called "the esteemed presence" of Premier Pham Van Dong—an associate of Ho Chi Minh's—to determine how best to rebuild it. Under the guidance and leadership of Nguyen Dinh Doan, the bridge was successfully reconstructed and rededicated. It provided a reliable river crossing and served the public until 2002. It is no longer used, however, to the extent it once was. Nearing the end of its useful life, the rusting steel frame of the Thanh Hoa Bridge still serves the railroad. Inspections are made of the rail on a monthly and some-times weekly basis.

Two men, using a template, measure the rail gauge to insure its proper width. They maintain a running, written record in a log book so as to spot any deficiencies with the rail width and the crossing and to identify any trends (severe corrosion not withstanding) that may be detrimental to the safety of crossing trains. Of course, the bridge still provides a river crossing for pedestrian and motorcycle traffic. The bridge that was once the focus of so much action, so much attention, a symbol of defiance, a rallying icon for the North Vietnamese during the sixties and early seventies stands silent, forlorn like an abandoned monument. Vehicular traffic now crosses the Song Ma via a nearby, newly constructed, pre-stressed concrete bridge de-signed by the Japanese. Drivers pay scant attention to the old rusting steel truss works just upstream of the new concrete bridge. Virtually forgotten, the majesty of the Thanh Hoa Bridge no longer commands awe. Seen from the new bridge downstream, Cau Ham Rong, the pride of Thanh Hoa, so fervently defended, has faded into history.

The USS *Kitty Hawk*, commissioned on April 29, 1961, converted from CVA-63 (Attack Carrier) to CV-63 (Multi-mission Carrier) in early 1973, underwent many extensive modifications over the years and continued its eminent service with the U.S. Navy in the Pacific and other oceans. Contin-uing its colorful history, *Kitty Hawk* was forward deployed to Yokosuka, Japan in 1998 and spent the next ten years operating from there. *Kitty Hawk* was a significant participant in the Iraq War and received many cita-tions. The final catapult shot from the deck of *Kitty Hawk* occurred on 6 August 2008. *Kitty Hawk* then returned to San Diego for its last visit to its original home port. The first and last operating carrier in its class, *Kitty Hawk*, was decommissioned during a well-attended ceremony on 31 January 2009 in Bremerton, Washington. She now lies moored next to her sister ship, USS *Constellation* (CV-64), now also decommissioned. Throughout her ser-vice at sea, *Kitty Hawk* received eighty-six distinguished awards.

Captains Todd A. Zecchin, a native of Detroit, Michigan, and Stephen J. Vissers were, respectively, the last Commanding Officer and Executive Offi-cer of *Kitty Hawk*. The last Command Master Chief was Charles A. Clarke.

The F-4B Phantom II that served as Linfield Two Zero One, that flew from the deck of *Kitty Hawk* on 14 May 1967, with the number 3001 writ-ten on its sides and the partial letters NH still visible on what remains of the vertical stabilizer (tail fin), now rests silently atop a specially made concrete structure within the grounds of the combined Vietnamese Air Defense and Air Force Museum on Truong Chinh Street in Hanoi. It was the six hundred twenty first Phantom made in St. Louis and had been in service one year prior to having been shot down. The F-4 Phantom II is covered with a green algae-looking patina, the result of years of sitting beneath a tree in the humid, wet Hanoi weather at its previous location just down the street.

Sitting impotently, amid other aircraft wreckage, the Phantom mocks a time when an American could not have stood on the same ground—near Bac Mai Airfield—a time when the thought of a U.S. warplane on display in North Vietnam could not even be imagined.

But it's there and it dominates the pile of U.S. aircraft debris that sits to each side of it, offering mute testimony to a much more violent time. The plane is intact, but that statement does not reveal what happened to it after it landed in the Ma River and little describes the current pitiful state of a once proud American aircraft that its visage now represents.

Closer inspection reveals how the Phantom was transported from the Ma River valley to Hanoi. Its engines removed, the Phantom's fuselage had been cut twice transversely resulting in three sections. The cuts were made behind the cockpit and just in front of the empennage. Its main wings were severed at the midsection of the wing spar and dropped individually. The Phantom was dissected into five sections total. What became of the Sparrow missiles it carried on 14 May 1967, or how the Vietnamese removed them, or what they did with them, may never be known.

To see what was once one of the most feared planes in the U.S. arsenal on such silent display is humbling. It's clearly an F-4, but it is a deceased, prehistoric creature—just a metallic carcass—truly a decaying, but sacred bird of war. Over the years, vandals have stripped Herman Barkey's proud warplane, flown by Ev Southwick, of its instruments, tubing, some sheet metal, wiring, and other parts. The only things remaining today that would be considered souvenirs, except the plane itself, are one throttle handle, the control stick and grip, and the RAT lever, all of which were at Ev Southwick's command decades before.

In striking juxtaposition, the Phantom sits surrounded by its archrivals: antiaircraft guns, SAM II and SAM III rockets, MiG-17s and MiG-21s.

There are many military museums in Hanoi and each one displays piles of debris from downed U.S. aircraft. The Army Museum displays bombs, cannons, and other captured American weaponry and a large array of virtually unidentifiable aircraft parts. But the combined Air Force and Air Defense Museum is the only museum to claim possession of an F-4 Phantom II.

About six hundred seventy F-4s were lost in Southeast Asia during the Vietnam conflict. During 1967, the worst year of the air war for the United States and the year with the heaviest losses of the F-4, the U.S. Air Force lost about one hundred F-4s and the U.S. Navy and U.S. Marines combined, a little more than fifty.

The F-4 Phantom II was relatively well exported by the US government. Purchased by several friendly foreign governments, though aging and suffering from lack of replacement parts, the Phantom still serves in their air forces today.

F-4 Phantom IIs would serve in the U.S. military in various forms through the 1990s and in limited roles into the new millennium. No longer a front line fighter jet, and a sad fact for many ex-pilots, F-4 Phantoms have been relegated to the role of drones serving as airborne targets. To many who flew it, though not all, the F-4 was a revered and cherished icon. Some pilots swore by the F-4, thought it the best aircraft they had ever flown and, when asked about flying it, became very descriptive through their animation; almost emotional. Others were less inspired, aloof, un-phased: "*It was an OK plane, I flew it. So what?*" one pilot stated stoically. For those with fond memories of the aircraft, the F-4 Phantom II Society preserves its heritage.

More than half a century after the flight of the first F-4, with their cockpits covered in a white, reflective coating, their engines, gyros, and various motors and pumps silent, their metallic skin tarnished in the desert sun, F-4 Phantom IIs have been placed side by side, row after row, at Davis-Monthan Air Force Base in Tucson, Arizona. They have met the end of their life and, all but forgotten, quietly await the fate of the scrap metal dealer.

The Collings Foundation, headquartered in Stow, Massachusetts, sought to preserve the heritage of the F-4 Phantom II. They recently restored an F-4D to full operational capabilities. Their privately owned Phantom is used for public flight demonstrations and is maintained at Ellington Field near Houston, Texas.

Elsewhere, with markings still visible on their fuselages, their organs removed, systems stripped, wires and panels hanging loose, abandoned F-4s sit ignoble, discarded in lonely, weed-infested bone yards, no longer wanted.

Yet, as witness to the achievement of a great design, taking its historical place alongside other legendary military aircraft, many F-4s have been mounted prominently atop memorial pedestals or put on proud display in museums across the United States. A comprehensive list of the location of every F-4 on display in the United States has been compiled. As of 2009, more than two hundred Phantoms were on static display around the United States. They are a majestic testament, a silent, unassuming declaration of a great era in aviation that is now passed.

Robert Bailey, a Canadian aviation artist, in 2004, created an excellent portrayal of an F-4 Phantom II during an attack on the Ham Rong Bridge. Entitled "Dragon Slayers," the dramatic painting depicts, in striking juxtaposition vis-à-vis the bridge, an F-4 Phantom II, also with the number 201 on its side but probably of Air Wing Fourteen (CVW-14), as it crosses above the bridge, just south and west of Nui Ngoc. The Phantom, flying in a northwest direction, followed by A-4 Skyhawks, has just unleashed its load of Zuni rockets. Please visit Mr. Bailey's website at *www.baileyprints.com*.

I attended the air show at Oshkosh in the summer of 2003 principally because I had heard an F-4 Phantom II would make an appearance. I have only seen the wreckage of an F-4—Linfield Two Zero One—and one other Phantom (BuNo 153016) now on loan from the U.S. Navy to the museum maintained by the Arizona Wing of the Commemorative Air Force in Mesa, Arizona, but I had never seen one fly. Oshkosh provided me with that opportunity.

On a very clear, Wisconsin day, I saw the Phantom's dark exhaust on the southern horizon as it made its approach just after I heard the radio communications between the pilot and the Oshkosh tower. When the Phantom came nearer, the spectators all rose to their feet to pay tribute to the famous fighter jet as it flashed overhead, its engines roaring. The Phantom was flown by USAF Major Mike Wilburn with Alex Mangold, of the German Luftwaffe, in the backseat. The aging but still proud F-4 belonged to the 20th Fighter Squadron (Silver Lobos), 49th Fighter Wing, a joint American/German flight training program at Holloman Air Force Base. The Phantom was eventually parked at Aero Shell Square near two NASA F-18 Hornets.

I was intrigued by the reaction of the spectators. They thronged the Phantom but paid little attention to the more modern F-18s that sat not more than two hundred feet away. Such is the continuing intrigue and mystique of Herman Barkey's F-4 Phantom II. There will never be another Phantom.

Afterword

I HAVE ALWAYS THOUGHT THE STORY OF the flight of Linfield Two Zero One should not be lost. Many people contributed to my efforts to relate this mini-history. Naively, I thought that the accounts would always agree, that one would support the other. They did not. The facts didn't always present themselves to me so neatly and cleanly. Additional research sometimes only confused the understanding and obscured the answers even more.

Once, when trying to trace the landing place of Ev and Jack's F-4, I met an elderly Vietnamese lady near Thanh Hoa and, through my translator, asked her if she recalled the day the Phantom fell from the sky. She said she did. She became lively as she sat in her tiny hut chewing beetle nut, her teeth and gums stained a deep red. She spoke rapidly with lots of gesturing. She explained what occurred in great detail. Entranced, I listened intently. I asked where the plane landed and she pointed just across the canal from where we were seated, not more than a hundred yards away. The translator told me that the plane was on fire and came straight down and crashed and exploded in flames and that only one pilot was seen descending in a parachute. Intrigued by this narrative but disappointed at the revelation, I knew it was not Ev and Jack's F-4. Their plane did not crash in flames.

On the same day, further into my search for the landing spot of the F-4, I experienced an almost surreal situation. The story of the landing of Ev and Jack's Phantom had been passed down through two generations and had grown almost to mythological proportions. As I proceeded along the levee of the Song Ma with my maps, people began pointing ahead of me. The gestures increased in number until I realized that word had spread among the villagers about my search for the landing place of Linfield Two Zero One. Everyone knew about the *Con ma*.

Another documented account: The day that Ev and Jack ejected from their stricken F-4, only one parachute opened, Ev's. Yet, the after-action reports noted "two good chutes." But because the person, Jack, whose parachute did not open, survived to tell about it, arrival at the logical conclusion was easy.

A report circulated on *Kitty Hawk* a few days after the loss of Linfield Two Zero One that photo interpreters thought the plane had been lifted and the landing gears extended. This seems unlikely and in any event, the main landing gears remain to this day retracted into their recessed bays beneath the giant wings.

And of course there is the claim of the number of American aircraft shot down while attacking the Thanh Hoa Bridge. Various Vietnamese accounts claim that anywhere from thirty to as many as three hundred planes were shot down. Beneath a MiG-17 on display in Vinh City, there sits a plaque that reads:

> MiG-17 Aircraft No. 2010—Tran Hanh Squadron, in coordination with antiaircraft artillery, militia, naval forces, shot down 47 U.S. Aircraft over Ham Rong, Thanh Hoa on April 3 and 4 1965.

The same claim of downing forty-seven American planes that were attacking the Ham Rong Bridge over the same two day period is made at the Air Force/Air Defense Museum in Hanoi by Trung Doan Phao Phong Khong 228 (Air Defense Artillery Regiment No. 228). This statistic is difficult to accept. Realistically speaking, if the North Vietnamese gunners (and pilots) were so accurate and deadly on any given day, why were they then not equally deadly on any other given day, especially when the bridge was attacked so often?

While the 3rd and 4th of April 1965 were significant days for American action against the Thanh Hoa Bridge, American loss records greatly differ. The raid on 3 April against the Thanh Hoa Bridge by the U.S. Air Force was planned and led by Lt. Col. Robinson Risner. The strike, involving dozens of F-105s and F-100s, resulted in the loss that day of an F-100D whose pilot was unable to eject after being hit by antiaircraft fire. He died when his jet crashed near the bridge. Risner's F-105 sustained damage and he was forced to land at Da Nang in South Vietnam.

Not far away, about ten miles north of the Thanh Hoa Bridge (and Thanh Hoa town), in an unrelated attack, the U.S. Navy lost an A-4C of VA-216 from the USS *Hancock* (CVA-19). The pilot ejected and was captured. While the loss of the A-4 and the F-100 were due to ground fire, MiG-17s were in action too and attacked and damaged an F-8 Crusader that landed at Da Nang.

A U.S. Air Force RF-101C was shot down on the 3rd in an unrelated mission farther south near Vinh.

But after the raids on 3 April, the Thanh Hoa Bridge was surprisingly still standing, not seriously damaged. On 4 April, Robinson Risner again led an attack against the Thanh Hoa Bridge but the strike encountered many problems. An F-105 was shot down probably by ground fire. Two other F-105s were lost and the pilots were killed. Another plane was also lost on 4 April. A Skyraider, an A-1H, was shot down, most likely by ground fire. The pilot was searching for the two airmen lost on the 3rd when his aircraft crashed near the bridge killing him.

In all, while six American planes were shot down near or in the immediate vicinity of the Thanh Hoa Bridge, only five American planes were shot down while in direct action against the bridge, including the search attempt by the A-1H Skyraider.

Of the one hundred twenty planes the North Vietnamese claim to have shot down over the Thanh Hoa Bridge, as purported in the museum display in Hanoi, Air Defense Artillery Regiment 228 claims to have shot down ninety of them. These statistics are unlikely. Even accounts from the American side vary to some degree but not to such an exaggerated extent or in such an embellished context.

In all, the Americans flew about 1,000 sorties against the Thanh Hoa Bridge, including the two special attacks by U.S. Air Force C-130s. While many planes were shot down in and around the vicinity of Thanh Hoa as a result of many various missions in the area, only a handful, a small percentage of American aircraft (some estimate ten or eleven) were lost while attacking the bridge or its air defenses. Ev Southwick and Jack Rollins, flying an F-4B with VF-114 from the USS *Kitty Hawk*, on 14 May 1967, were among them and may have been the last U.S. airmen to be downed while striking the bridge or its air defenses.

There were many such oddities and contradictions; and to wade through them and make sense of them was frustrating more often than not. But the research was at all times intriguing and captivating.

Linfield Two Zero One was not the only American plane lost in the skies over Vietnam or elsewhere over Southeast Asia on 14 May 1967. Other losses included a U.S. Air Force F-104C from Udorn Air Base that crashed in Thailand and an F-105D from Korat Air Base that was shot down by a SAM and crashed near Laos. An F-100D from Bien Hoa air base was shot down over the Mekong Delta. Each incident has its own unique story.

Finally, I have tried to present the facts and sequence of events of the flight of Linfield Two Zero One and other contributing elements of the story in a readable manner as best I can reconstruct them from what documents and oral histories are available to me.

Appendix

AIR WING ELEVEN (CVW-11), ON ITS NOVEMBER 1966-June 1967 cruise to the Gulf of Tonkin, under the command of CDR Henry Urban, was comprised of the following squadrons, detachments and aircraft type:

Squadron	Aircraft Type
VF-114	F-4
VF-213	F-4
VA-85	A-6
VA-112	A-4
VA-144	A-4
VAW-114	E-2A
RVAH-13	RA-5C
VAH-4 Det C	KA-3B
HC-1 D1 Unit C	UH-2A and UH-2B
VAP-61 Det	RA-3B
VQ-1 Det	EA-3B

Total combat sorties from *Kitty Hawk*: est. 10,500

Total ordnance dropped by Air Wing Eleven: est. 2,000,000 pounds

Total air victories: 4 (2 AN-2 Colts and 2 MiG-17s)

Total air losses by aircraft type: F-4 (6); A-4 (3); A-6 (3); RA-5C (2); A-3 (1)

Last catapult launch of cruise from deck of *Kitty Hawk*: 18 June 1967, off the coast of San Diego.

VF-114, under the command of CDR Henry L. Halleland, arrived at NAS Miramar on 18 June 1967.

About the Author

GARY WAYNE FOSTER, SEEN HERE SITTING on a 2,000 pound bomb found near the Thanh Hoa Bridge, has written numerous professional articles for engineering publications. A comprehensive account of his experiences in India has been translated into the Bengali language and published internationally. He is a frequent contributor to *Red Clay* magazine, the official publication of the Khe Sanh Veterans Association. His professional assignments have taken him to many countries including India, Vietnam, Bosnia, Jamaica, Cambodia, China, Bolivia, El Salvador, Afghanistan, Kazakhstan, Liberia and Congo, as well as other parts of Africa, and Iraq. He holds a BS degree in Civil Engineering from the University of California at Davis, an MS degree from the University of Alaska and an MBA from The George Washington University. He is a registered professional engineer in Idaho, California and the District of Columbia. In addition to his years living in India, he has also lived in New Zealand, Australia, Zaire (Democratic Republic of Congo) and France. A native of Oklahoma, raised in North Carolina, Arizona and California, he currently serves as Vice President with Stanley Consultants headquartered in Muscatine, Iowa.